Southold
Reminiscences

JOSEPH NELSON HALLOCK
This portrait of Joseph Nelson Hallock is after the painting by his son-in-law, Thomas
Currie-Bell. It was used when Hallock served as honorary chairman of Southold's
Anniversary Celebration.

Southold
Reminiscences

RURAL AMERICA AT THE TURN OF THE CENTURY

JOSEPH NELSON HALLOCK

GEOFFREY K. FLEMING, Editor

Charleston   London

THE
History
PRESS

Published by The History Press
Charleston, SC 29403
www.historypress.net

Front cover: Joseph and Ella Hallock and their friends put a lot of youthful energy into their annual "Two Days' Sail" excursions, with overnights at nearby ports like Montauk or New London, where "enough food would be taken to feed a multitude." In 1901, Joseph's sister Lucy and friend Minnie Smith prepared a scrapbook, with captions and sketches, to commemorate the event. *Courtesy of the Southold Free Library.*

First published 2008

Manufactured in the United States

ISBN 978.1.59629.546.9

Library of Congress Cataloging-in-Publication Data
Hallock, Joseph N. (Joseph Nelson), 1861-1942.
   Southold reminiscences : rural America at the turn of the century / Joseph N. Hallock ;
Geoffrey Fleming, editor.
      p. cm.
   Includes bibliographical references and index.
   ISBN 978-1-59629-546-9
   1. Southold (N.Y. : Town)--Social life and customs--19th century. 2. Southold (N.Y. : Town)-
-History--19th century. 3. City and town life--New York (State)--Southold (Town)--History-
-19th century. 4. Country life--New York (State)--Southold (Town)--History--19th century.
5. Hallock, Joseph N. (Joseph Nelson), 1861-1942--Childhood and youth. 6. Southold (N.Y.
: Town)--Biography. 7. Southold (N.Y.)--History--19th century. I. Fleming, Geoffrey K. II.
Title.
   F129.S74H25 2008
   974.7'25--dc22
                              2008024604

Notice: The information in this book is true and complete to the best of our knowledge. It is offered without guarantee on the part of the author or The History Press. The author and The History Press disclaim all liability in connection with the use of this book.

Contents

CONTENTS

CONTENTS

Map of Southold (Beers Atlas)
The Hallock homestead is clearly marked on Great Hog Neck (lower middle part of the map) under the name "G. Hallock."

Foreword

When in the fall of 1937, at the behest of his daughter Ann, Joseph Nelson Hallock began his memoirs, he had no intention, he said, of their being published.

> *I shall make no attempt at finished style in composition,* [he wrote,] *and I fear there will be little continuity in my narrative of events…My only object is to give my daughter, and any other friends interested, a glimpse of by-gone days.*

Perhaps. But Joseph Hallock had spent most of his life in the public eye, including three terms in the state legislature, decades as a trustee and president of the Southold Board of Education and Southold Savings Bank and twenty-five years as Southold town clerk. Furthermore, his career was in publishing, including thirty-eight years as the head of the country newspaper, the *Long Island Traveler*. In addition, his wife, Ella Boldry Hallock (1861–1934), was a noted author, editor and the first American translator of *Grimm's Fairy Tales*. With this rich background, it is hard to imagine his not taking a longer view of his writing.

As he began to write, his daughter, Ann Currie-Bell (1897–1964), was writing too—in her diary. Four times she mentioned his project, and her entries throw light on both the process and its reception. On October 9, 1937, she wrote:

> *Pop and I stayed home together. Pop got on to telling me about the old Bay View days, the district school, domino parties for men only & refreshments were always hard cider and apples!*

By October 16, he had begun: "Pop writing his memoirs for me as I had begged him to do." On November 12, she wrote:

> *Poppie is so delighted over writing his recollections of his life, and they are most valuable—describing his era in town life—Old Bay View & his boyhood days, the coming of Momie into his life, the customs, and work, and play (some, not much)—and the flavor of Southold in its village growth.*

And on December 17:

> *Had a fine party…Dominoes, games & Bingo…Pop read some of his recollections which delighted everyone—the choice part of the whole party. Peggy said they were more appealing than Mary Ellen Chase's & ought to be published.*

Chase (1887–1973), a native of Maine, had followed a similar track in her writing, reminiscing about the days of her youth and early life in her small coastal town of Blue Hill, which she documented in her autobiographical works, *A Goodly Heritage* (1932), *A Goodly Fellowship* (1939) and *The White Gate: Adventures in the Imagination of a Child* (1954).

Comparison of Hallock to such a celebrated American author (and winner of the Hale Award) must have made a strong impression on both Ann and her father. Publishing these stories as a companion to earlier histories, such as *Griffin's Journal* (1857), *Whitaker's Southold* (1881) and *Southold's Celebration* (1890), was logical. Together they would provide some of the most detailed accounting of who had lived and what had happened in Southold Town during its first three hundred years.

But these stories of life in Southold were destined to be hidden away for more than a generation. The Tercentenary Celebration (which Joseph Hallock chaired and for which Ann wrote a book) took place in 1940 and diverted everyone's attention from the memoir. Hallock himself died in 1942, and his daughter Ann suffered the loss of her husband, the noted painter Thomas Currie-Bell, just a few years later in 1946.

With little income or money at the end of her life, it became nearly impossible for Ann to publish her father's memoirs during her lifetime. Never one to falter, Ann threw herself into many community activities, including what was then called the "Historical Committee" of the Southold-Peconic Civic Association. It is out of this association that Ann and others would eventually found the Southold Historical Society, where she would serve as the first president (1960–64). It would be at the society that this manuscript would eventually come to rest, donated by Ann to become a part of the growing archival holdings.

Even though the memoir was now secure at the society, Hallock's manuscript would be largely forgotten by succeeding historians and society insiders, sitting decade after decade in a storage box. With many focused on studying the settlement and colonial era, there seemed little interest in the more "recent" history of the area. It was not until the early 1990s that the manuscript was even mentioned as existing in the archive, and even then it took another ten years for anyone within the society to recognize its significance to local history.

The rediscovery of the manuscript has made it possible for many of us to catch a glimpse, for the first time, of what daily life was like in Southold during the second half of the nineteenth and the first half of the twentieth centuries. And not only does it include historical facts and dates, but also information that details the everyday and annual activities that were part of life then; activities such as having to travel from the four corners of the town (by foot, horse or cart) to vote in Southold hamlet, where annual elections were held. We cannot comprehend such activities today as we walk to the local school or firehouse to vote.

Despite Joseph Hallock's protestations about its unfinished nature, we have made very few changes to his original manuscript. The order, spellings, capitalizations and grammar are his, as are the frequent and charming section headings. Commas and paragraphs (he had hardly any) *have* been added—for clarification and for the sake of the reader. Sentences that would otherwise go on for more than a page in some instances are now a great deal easier to read and understand.

Joseph Hallock was born in 1861 and spent the first twenty years of his life as a farm boy. It was, as he says, a life in which everything was done by hand and without the aid of running water or electricity. In 1937, five years before his death, he took those things for granted, as well as the radio, telephone, movies and the automobile. "No," he concluded, "we would not want to go back to the former days, much as we recall them with fond recollection." Nor, no doubt, would we. But it is fascinating to read about them. In any event, we are sure he would be pleased with this publication— almost seventy years later.

In preparing this manuscript for publication, a great deal of editing, researching and just plain old transcription work had to be completed. This work is often extremely time-consuming and even more often boring, to say the least. In addition to myself, it is important to recognize others whose contributions have made the publishing of Hallock's memoir not just a dream, but a reality.

Many thanks to the former chair of the Archives Committee, Clara Bjerknes, who initially helped record the memoir's existence in our archive and supported the further exploration of having it published. And a very special thanks to Society Trustee Helen Didriksen, one of the volunteers who works regularly in the society's archive. Helen spent hours transcribing the original manuscript and worked with me to research questionable words and phrases, documented sources and helped to determine which photographs would become part of the final product. Without her hard work and diligence this book would not have made it to press.

Geoffrey K. Fleming
Director, Southold Historical Society
Summer 2008

Reminiscences of "By-Gone Days"

By Joseph N. Hallock, 1937

This is not an autobiography, but at the request of my daughter, Ann Hallock Currie-Bell, I will attempt to jot down incidents connected with my life. There is an old saying that "the old live in the past, and the young in the future." In writing these memoirs, I shall make no attempt at finished style in composition, and I fear there will be little continuity in my narrative of events as I ask you to walk with me down Memory's Lane. My only object is to give my daughter, and any other friends interested, a glimpse of by-gone days.

My Birth

The Family Bible says that I was born at Bay View (then Hog Neck) on Sept. 16, 1861. I have no recollection of the event, but as I was taught that everything in the Good Book was true, I assume the date is correct. I was the son of George and Maria Jane (Dickinson) Hallock. I am told that I can claim descent from two of the original settlers of Southold in 1640—Peter Hallock (Peter, William, Thomas, Zerrubabel, Joseph, Joseph, George) and Philemon Dickinson. I was blessed by having both my father and mother live until I was of middle-age. I shall never forget the great debt I owe them for my upbringing. My father was one of the sweetest-tempered men I ever knew, and his name was a synonym for rugged honesty and square-dealing with his fellow-men. My mother attained the good old age of 95 years, with all her faculties unimpaired, and she was a blessing to all who knew her. I had four sisters and two brothers, only one of whom remains, Lucy Hallock Folk.

My Homes

My father was a farmer and owned large farm lands and woods at Bay View, and I worked on his farm until I was 21 years old. The old Hallock

THE OLD HALLOCK HOMESTEAD, THEN AND "NOW"

In 1861, when Joseph Hallock was born in this house (on the north side of Main Bayview Road, just east of Midland Parkway), it was a fairly modest structure (top). By the time he wrote his memoirs in 1937, it had doubled in size and was owned by the Akscin family (bottom). It still stands.

THE HALLOCK FARM OF JOSEPH'S BOYHOOD
When Joseph was four, his father traded his farm for land a quarter of a mile to the west, and it is this that became the locus of his childhood memories. The farmhouse still stands, just east of the North Fork Sign Company.

homestead was on what is now the William Akscin farm, but the house has been remodeled and enlarged in recent years.[1] When I was four years old my father traded his farm for the Albert Terry farm, about a quarter of a mile to the west. This is now owned by the heirs of Howard Terry.[2] I have but faint recollections of the home where I was born. I remember being placed on a mule's back and ingloriously falling off in the dirt. I also remember a play-house that I had under the large brick-oven, and a long room in the house where I was held in my mother's lap. I can recollect the ride I had for my first visit to my new home, when, with the help of our neighbors, we moved. And that sums up all I remember of the place where I was born.

School Life

I was taught my alphabet, how to read a little and do small sums in addition by my mother before I entered the little Bay View district school at the age of six.[3] That school I attended until I was 15 years old, when I finished my education by three winters at Southold Academy,[4] under Prof. James R. Robinson, who later became a Presbyterian minister.

At first I went to school both winter and summer, but when I became old enough to do work on the farm—and that was at an early age, for they had no compulsory school law in those days—I only went to school winters. I remember one of my summer teachers was Mary Curtis, now Mrs. George Henry Terry, and she was an excellent teacher. They would have a man to teach winters and a young lady wielded the birch in the summers. The girls attended school the year round, but the boys exited school in the spring, when farm work began, and did not go again until farm work was completed about the middle of November. The last farm work in the fields

BAY VIEW SCHOOL
The one-room schoolhouse that Joseph attended from ages six to fifteen was just a stone's throw from his home, across the road and just east of the Jacob's Lane triangle. It has since been moved to the Southold Historical Society's Main Road complex.

was carting up the corn-stalks, after the corn was husked in the lot. On Saturdays we went in the woods to cut wood, and when that was done and carted home, we would saw with a hand-saw and split wood and cut up refuse wood at the woodpile. We had plenty of wood and burned no coal in those days. One sign of winter was the moving of the cook-stove from the kitchen to the sitting room.

My uncle, J. Nelson Dickinson, who lived with us, was generally hired as teacher for the winter months. He was an excellent teacher and a strict disciplinarian and could handle the big, unruly boys. He very seldom used the rod. One of his punishments was to make the bad boys sit under the teacher's desk, "out of sight of all good people," as he said, and yet the culprit could be seen by all the pupils. It was not a very comfortable position, as the desk was low and the offender could not sit up straight. Another punishment was making the pupil stand up for some time with his or her face to the wall. If one did not learn his lessons, he had to stay after school to learn them, and sometimes the kerosene lamp had to be lighted before the task was done. A frequent punishment was making the pupil stay in at both the morning and afternoon recess of 15 minutes, sometimes for a week if the offense was particularly bad. This was indeed a hardship when one

J. NELSON DICKINSON
J. Nelson Dickinson was both Joseph Hallock's uncle and schoolteacher, being hired by the Bay View School during the winter months (when the boys attended). He also lived with Joseph's family.

could hear his fellows playing ball. A frequent reason for punishment was whispering, which was strictly forbidden.

Another man teacher I went to was George Horton Terry. My best beloved teacher was Carrie Huntting, though I thought very much of Carrie Hutchinson. Julia Williamson was another teacher. The last winter I attended Bay View School I went to Sylvester Tuthill.

The old school house had a huge wood-stove, and one would roast if he got near it, and the temperature was far below 70 if you sat in the back part of the room, and that is where the big scholars sat, the Primary children being in front, the girls on one side of the room and the boys on the other. Sometimes, if a scholar was particularly bad, he or she was made to sit on a front seat, so as to be under the eagle eye of the teacher. It was comical to see a big boy or girl sitting with the little tots.

The desks and benches were hand-made, and the benches had no backs to them. Long recitation benches were in front. The only chair in the room was the teacher's chair. The tops of the desks were cut up in great shape, generally with the pupils' initials. Sometimes a small hole would be cut in the desk and a piece of glass fitted over it, and one would catch flies and put them in their prison. There were no fly-screens in the windows then. It was a proud day for us when the old desks and benches were thrown out and cut up for firewood, and second-hand desks and chairs installed in their place. Some who did not have children to send to school thought this was a needless expense and would make taxes higher. After the new furniture was installed, there was no longer any carving of desks, and the flies lived on.

We were grounded in the essentials of "readin', writin', spellin' and 'rithmetic." Every winter when we entered school we would begin at Addition and get a little farther in the book each year. Long Division and Fractions were the great stumbling blocks in our scholastic careers. Every one in school had to read, from the First to the Sixth Reader. How we loved to read the good old selections, and with what sonorous sound they came from our lips. When it came time for writing, everyone brought out his or her copy-book. I can well remember the uplifting Proverbs we copied. The first one or two lines we copied would be pretty good, but as we got farther and farther down the page the writing would greatly deteriorate, for we were copying our own handwriting instead of the neat and legible copy at the top.

Spelling was made much account of, and we had spelling lessons each day and spelling matches once a week. One way was to stand in two opposite rows, the teachers choosing the spellers, and when one missed a word he would have to sit down, or else he would go to the foot of the other side. At the end of a certain time, the side having the most standing would win. The other way was for all to stand in one line, the leader choosing his fellow-pupils one by one. When one missed a word, the one spelling it correctly would take his place as the one who missed the word would either go to his seat or to the front of the class.

One of the things eagerly sought for was the chance to pass the water for the other thirsty pupils. You had to take the water-pail over to Uncle Austin Horton's to fill it up, for there was no pump at the school house, though later one was driven. You would often hear the request, with uplifted hand, "Please, Teacher, my I pass the water?" It is passing strange how much water those pupils could drink. The cup of course was first passed to the teacher. All drank from the same cup. Germs had not been heard of then.

The great day of the week was Friday afternoon. Then we would have our literary exercises, and every pupil, except the very youngest, had to either "speak a piece" or write and read an essay. The essays were marvels of composition, and the walls fairly shook as the young orators declaimed. Woe to the scholar who "played hookey"—he had to pay dearly for his fun. In the winter there were as high as sixty scholars in the one small room, all taught by the one teacher—from the one learning his Alphabet to the advanced scholar in the Sixth Reader.

I remember that once the school had a public entertainment in the evening and charged ten cents admission. Music was furnished by Lewis Freeman, colored, and Hector Horton on their fiddles. Needless to say, the music was not classical, but the audience enjoyed the old, familiar tunes. We sang songs and there were several dialogues and declamations. The school house was packed. There was only one door, and the audience had to walk over the stage to get to the seats. It was a great night. The training I received in speaking at that little school house came in good stead when I became an amateur actor.

We suppose the teaching in the "little red school houses" would be considered crude and certainly out-of-date now, but the pupils acquired a fine foundation. The pupils, though they learned the Alphabet in the old-fashioned way, could make many a college graduate of today hang his head in shame when it came to reading correctly, spelling, writing, geography and figuring correctly.

School Meetings

The annual school meetings at Bay View were well attended and were highly exciting affairs. They were generally fought out on the question of whether or not my uncle, J. Nelson Dickinson, should be hired to teach the winter session of the school. He wanted $8.00 a week, and a lady teacher could be hired for $6.00 or $7.00. Most always the partisans of my uncle won, for the majority of the voters thought it was necessary to have a man teacher to handle the big boys, who only attended the school during the winter, even if it did add a few cents to their tax. For the most part, those who objected to paying the extra tax sent no children to school.

Southold Academy

When I was 15 years old I entered Southold Academy, which I attended for three winters, and that ended my scholastic career. I feel that I owe a great deal to my training at the Academy. First, we were taught to be young gentlemen and ladies. I there became fired with an ambition to improve my mind and make something of myself. I acquired the habit of reading biography, history and the best in literature, and that love of reading has staid with me to this day.

There were no bicycles or automobiles in my Academy days, and I would make the three-mile journey on-foot from my home and return the same way at night. Sometimes I would catch a ride with some friendly soul. I never wore an overcoat, even in the coldest weather, with the thermometer registering near zero. When I was at the Academy I took a great interest in my Latin, and after I had left I continued my studies in that subject with Mrs. Mattie Wells as tutor. Mattie was a graduate of the Academy and a very fine Latin scholar. Alas! I fear I could not read correctly a Latin sentence now.

SOUTHOLD ACADEMY

Joseph's last three years of schooling were spent here. He walked the three miles each way to Horton's Lane and "never wore an overcoat." Academy Printing now occupies the building.

ACADEMY INTERIOR

The interior is shown decorated for the 1890 celebration. On the wall is a portrait of Deacon Moses Conklin Cleveland, painted by Orlando Hand Beers.

SOUTHOLD ACADEMY REUNION, 1940
Joseph Hallock stands (front row, right), hat in hand, at his Southold Academy graduating class's sixtieth reunion.

Farm Work

I will now go back to the work and life on my father's farm. As soon as I was old enough—and that was early, for boys were not coddled in those days—I went to work. There were no light-hour days then.[5] Soon after sunrise I was called up out of bed and went out to milk our four cows and feed the stock. Then I sat down to a big breakfast of ham or sausage and griddle-cakes. We always took a lunch down-lot to eat at 10 o'clock, then home at noon to eat a big dinner, which was the big meal of the day, and then a good supper at night. As a general thing we would eat again just before going to bed—the menu being a sparerib sandwich, mince-pie and similar light refreshments. And we were so tired from our day's work on the farm that we would go to sleep as soon as we touched the bed and sleep like a top until called all-too-soon to get up and milk the cows. We often worked in the field until near sundown.

HAY WAGON
"The work on the farm was all done by hand-work in the 'good old days,'" recalled Joseph. Here, farmworkers load up the hay wagon.

My father, like all other farmers in those days, planted varied crops—potatoes, corn, wheat, oats, hay, etc. What wheat we did not sell we took to the mill to have ground into flour. We raised pigs for ourselves and feasted on salt and fresh pork, home-cured ham and sausage, which my mother stuffed in long bags and hung up in the attic. We would always depend on selling enough pigs to pay the taxes. We would kill a beef and sour the forequarter to make corn-beef of, and the hind-quarter, which brought a better price, we sold to the butcher. We had a large flock of hens, and we would trade the eggs not used in the family for groceries. As a matter of fact, they paid for all the groceries used.

When the minister and his wife or friends came to dinner, my mother would invariably have a pair of fowl killed for dinner. I should have thought the poor minister would never have wanted to look a chicken in the face, for every parishioner followed the example of my mother, and the pastors were great on making pastoral calls in those days.

We never had to buy fertilizer, and that was unheard of then, for our stock made enough, and then, too, we caught thousands of bunkers to throw on the land. There was no Town Ordinance then making one cover up the fish, and as one rode by the fields the stench rose to high heaven. We had a fish-pound, which we set in the spring, and had to get up at 3 o'clock in the morning to tend it. This early rising was necessary, because we caught a good many "good-fish," mostly weak-fish, and these we shipped to Fulton Fish Market. The freight train left Southold at 9 a.m., and we had to drive a mile to the net, raise it, take out and sort the fish, take them to the ice-house to ice, box them, and then drive the three miles to the railroad station before the train left for New York. Sometimes if there was a glut of fish in the market, the returns were very meager—perhaps a few postage-stamps instead of the check we hoped for. The bunkers which we did not need we sold to neighboring farmers for $1.50 a thousand. Jesse Terry, Will Beebe and myself had a draw-seine and we would go nights and draw it, either at Cedar Beach or Paradise Point. Sometimes we would not get home before 10 p.m., and that made a mighty short time for sleep when one had to get up at 3 o'clock the next morning. During the fishing season we feasted on weak-fish twice a day—for dinner and supper.

There were plenty of scallops and soft and hard crabs in those days, as well as eels and crabs in Goose, Cedar Beach and Corey's Creeks. One had only to go down to the Bay after a hard blow and pick up several bushels of scallops. We took them home and opened them in the kitchen, and I became quite expert in opening the delicious bivalves. I never could keep a shell in the air all the time as some could. They would make good money opening them for market. The scallops sold for 20 cents a quart. It was no trouble to go down to the shore at low tide and dig a big mess of soft clams. Hard clams were in the bays and creeks for the raking. For eels, we would either go "fire-lighting" at night or spear them through the ice. One could come home with a bushel of crabs. "Horse-feet" were made much account of, to open and feed to the pigs and hens. We would pole a boat along the shore at night, when it was high tide, and spear the king-crabs as they came ashore to bed.

On the first day of August we would go down to the creek to pull creek-mud, and this task would last for three weeks. This was either done by tongs to wind around the long sea-weed, or with a large, long-handled rake to scoop up the seaweed and some mud. It was hard work, but we boys would enjoy it. Every time we changed our clothes—for we had to wear old clothes for this work (and how wet and cold they were when we put them on, for they had been hanging on the fence all night)—we would take a swim in the muddy creek and, when we were done, would go and catch a mess of crabs. We pulled the seaweed on large floats. When we had a load, we would pole ashore and pitch it on a long, narrow heap as high as one's head. There it would remain until winter, when we would

SEINING, CIRCA 1920

These Southolders are performing a common activity of Joseph's boyhood: seining, or pulling in pre-placed nets to remove the fish captured in them. They are identified as the "Champion Fishing Club," and Albert T. Dickerson, Henry Wines and Albert W. Albertson are among them.

cart it home and unload it in heaps, and there it would remain until spring, when we would spread it and plow it under for corn. It made an excellent fertilizer for this crop.

The bay-seaweed that drove up on our beach after a hard storm we would cart up and put in the pig-pens. We aimed not to put this on potato ground when we carted it out in the spring, for if we did so it would make the potatoes grubby. Then the bays and creeks were full of seaweed. Now, for some reason which I do not know, there is hardly a trace of it. The first farm work we did in the spring was to clean out the pig-pens and cow-yard.

By the way, the only value that the farmer put on bay-front property was the privilege of getting seaweed. For all other purposes it was worthless, unless it was a place to go swimming from. They never thought of building a house on the shore. They wanted to be on the main road.

We always rotated our crops. We would never have thought of planting a crop year after year on the same piece of ground, as they plant potatoes today. First, the grass ground was plowed for corn, to be followed by potatoes, then wheat (timothy and clover being sown with the wheat), then hay and, last, pasture for the horses and cows. Then we would commence the process all over again.

I can well remember the first cauliflower we raised—one-quarter acre—and we received over a hundred dollars for it. The cauliflower we would always trim and pack in barrels at night, by the light of a lantern. Then we would cart it to Southold in the morning for the early freight train. I can remember the first commercial fertilizer we bought—Mapes, two bags of it. What would our farmers think today of buying that quantity?

I can also well remember the first potato-bug that appeared on our potato vines. We did not know what they were, but later read in the paper that they came from Colorado, where they were a great pest. At first we tried to cope with them by picking them off in a tin-can, then burning them in kerosene. But they multiplied by the million faster than we could pick them off. Then we mixed Paris green with water and used a sprinkling-pot to sprinkle the deadly mixture on the potato vines, and that proved a very effective exterminator.

For my own particular piece of ground my father gave me a quarter-acre of the best land on which to raise onions. I can still remember the back-ache I had in weeding those onions. I wonder if that has anything to do with the fact that the onion is the one vegetable that I cannot eat to-day. I wore out more than one pair of pants in crawling on my hands and knees as I weeded the onions. If the pants were not worn out entirely, my mother would put a big patch on each knee. It was no unusual sight to see patched clothes in those days.

When I had gathered the onions, I would take them with the horse and farm-wagon to Greenport and peddle them out. I remember that more than once I almost got stuck in the sloughs of mud at Arshamomoque.[6] Very little was done to the roads in those days, one simply had to get through them one way or another. Sometimes the wheels would go down to the axles in mud. Though it was an awful lot of work to raise those onions, it was quite a profitable crop, and I was able to buy a $10.00 suit of Sunday-go-to-meeting clothes and some other necessaries, and put a few dollars in "Henry Huntting's Savings Bank."[7]

The work on the farm was all done by hand-work in the "good old days." There was no farm machinery except a mower and reaper. I have dug thousands of bushels of potatoes with a pitch-fork. The first potato-digger I saw was manufactured by D.Y. Hallock. My father tried it, put preferred the pitch-fork. We very seldom sold potatoes out of the lot. We would put them in

THE HUNTTING HOUSE, FIRST HOME OF SOUTHOLD SAVINGS BANK
(FOUNDED 1858)
The first home of the Southold Savings Bank was in the house of Edward Huntting, brother of its treasurer, Henry Huntting. So completely did Joseph Hallock equate the institution and the man that he talked about putting his boyhood savings into "Henry Huntting's Savings Bank."

the cellar and cart them out in the spring. The price we received was about 50 cents a bushel, though I remember one year when we only received 15 cents.

We had a number of white ox-heart cherry trees on our place, and it was my job to pick the fruit. I made no objection, for I took a pretty big toll. Those cherries tasted mighty good, and I swallowed a fair number of pits. I must have had a good digestive apparatus, for I was never troubled with indigestion, and the pits could not have caused any permanent injury, for it is nearly seventy years since I swallowed them.

Martin Gordon had a huge mulberry tree and he told me to come and pick all the mulberries I wanted. I accepted the invitation, and what I did not eat I took home to my mother to make pies of.

I used to go down to the pond to catch big bull-frogs. After killing them, I would take off and skin the legs, and when they were fried they made mighty fine eating. When I am eating swell-fish I think of those frogs' legs, for their taste is very similar. Speaking of swell-fish, in after years when I went fishing I always had to bring some swell-fish home to Ella, for she liked them better than any other fish.

—⚶—

Bay View Roads

Speaking of D.Y. Hallock reminds me of the great fight he had with his neighbors at Bay View, then Hog Neck, over the roads. Mr. Hallock was not a native; he had moved here from Northville, and the old-timers keenly resented his coming here and telling them how to build roads. No matter if he could trace his lineage back to the same Puritan ancestry as themselves, he was an outsider. They could point to generation after generation born at Hog Neck. The roads which were good enough for their fathers were good enough for them.

There was a great half-moon stretch of road in front of Mr. Hallock's farm that always banked up with snow. Mr. Hallock owned land to the south of the road, including a deep ditch, and he proposed to fill in the ditch and lay out a straight road on the south, and of course take the old road in his farm. Then the fight was on. It was taken before the Road Commissioners and counsel was employed. Mr. Hallock won, and the new road was laid out, as it is today. All now recognize that that was the right decision on the part of the Commissioners, but they did not then.

Again Mr. Hallock ran up against his neighbors when he proposed to cut down Brushes' Hill and make it much easier of ascent.[8] The road was sandy and steep, and in carting produce to market one had to load with the tough climb of Brushes' Hill in mind. Again Mr. Hallock won, and again he was right. I was a small boy at the time, but hearing my father and the neighbors talking together, I became a strong partisan for their side.

The matter had political repercussions. Jonathan B. Terry, who was one of the Road Commissioners who had decided in favor of Mr. Hallock, became the Republican candidate for Supervisor of Southold Town. He was only defeated by eight votes, and those votes were cast by his Republican cousins in Hog Neck, who had never before voted a Democratic ticket. My father, who was a very strong Republican, never having voted a Democratic ticket, and a warm personal friend of Mr. Terry, would not follow the lead of his neighbors, and voted for Mr. Terry.

Apples and Cider

Like most of the farmers, my father had a large apple orchard, and I can taste those Russets, Baldwins, Greenings, Bellflowers and Granny-Payne's now. We always feasted on them just before going to bed, with a glass of cider to wash them down. My mother said that "an apple a day kept the doctor away." To be sure that the one-apple preventative worked, we added several more of the same dose.

In the evening, the whole family would join in peeling, coring and slicing apples in about one-eights. These we placed on a board and put them on the flat tin-roof over the kitchen, covering them with mosquito netting to keep off the flies, so that they would dry in the sun. Dried apple, cooked with sugar or molasses, was the principal fruit we had for dessert, though my

J.B. Terry
Owner of the wharf, Terry was also heavily involved in town politics. He served as a road commissioner and was defeated for the town supervisor's post by one of the tightest margins (eight votes) ever.

mother always put up several big earthen jars of pickled peaches, plums and pears, and they were a welcome change from the diet of dried apples.

My mother was a great cook, though she never went by a recipe-book, and she would bake great batches of bread, biscuits, sugar and molasses (mostly molasses) cookies, rice pudding and pies galore. Will I ever forget those great jars full of twisted (not round) crullers? We lived well. There was no stinting our stomachs. In the berrying time, we would go and bring home big, 10-quart pails of blackberries and huckleberries. A favorite place to pick blackberries was the big open lot surrounding "The Bandbox."[9] After going in the woods to pick huckleberries, we would always go in swimming to wash off the little bugs that would get on us. Those pesky critters would make one itch to beat the band.

My father had a cider-mill, and in addition to making our own cider, the neighbors would come there and grind their apples. For this service they paid one-cent a gallon. The boys, with a straw, would suck the sweet cider from the mill. They said it was as good as a dose of physic. Everyone drank hard-cider in those days, and I drank my full share of it. The doctors said it was the best remedy for dyspepsia. I don't remember ever having that ailment, but I guess I must have drank the cider as a preventative. "An ounce of prevention is worth a pound of cure," they say, and I sure drank plenty of ounces. However, I only drank one glass at a time and was never under the influence of liquor to my knowledge. I still love a glass of cider, and I will confess that I want some tang to it.

SOUTHOLD BAY SWIMMING PARTY
In Joseph Hallock's boyhood, swimming was one of the few leisure pastimes. His sister Lucy took part in this swimming party in the early 1900s.

—◁ʍ▷—

Samp Porridge

I was always very fond of samp porridge. In the good old days, we did not buy ready-made samp, as we do to-day. We went to "Peter Gil" Wells, who had a large pestle and mortar, the same as the Indians used, only this pestle was suspended from a suspended long stick, and there we pounded the husks off the corn. I can now taste that samp porridge as my mother used to make it. The ingredients were samp, beans, potatoes, turnips, salt pork, a beef-bone, pickled pigs' hocks (which were especially tasty) and sometimes, if we wanted it extra good, a chicken. It had to be boiled for hours and carefully watched and stirred, so that it would not burn. I always wanted my heaping soup-plate filled up again. That was a dish fit for a king! This is a purely New England dish, handed down from the Puritans. When Ella came here from up-State she had never heard of it (samp alone was used), and she was very fond of it.

—◁ʍ▷—

Stealing Watermelons

As a boy, I was never guilty of stealing anything more than apples and watermelons, and there was no sense in that, for we had plenty of each. Perhaps because other boys would steal from us, I wanted to retaliate in kind. One dark night, I, in company with another boy, Jot Overton, went to "Peter Gil" Wells' melon patch to hook a watermelon. What I thought was a cat ran by my legs, but unfortunately for my clothes it was no pussy, but a skunk! I was well perfumed, and it was weeks before I could wear that suit after it had been hung out for the wind to blow through it. I have <u>never stolen a watermelon since</u>. To this day, I am more afraid of a skunk than I am of a lion. I will plead a little justification for my sin by stating that I was never guilty of taking but one melon at a time, and I never smashed any.

Creek-Thatch

One work on the farm, handed down from the days of our forefathers in 1640, was the cutting of creek-thatch on the salt meadows. This, after being cured in the lot, was carted in the barn and fed to the stock. I question whether there was much nourishment in it, but the animals liked it on account of the salt taste.

Most of the Bay View farmers had a certain number of rights in "The Commoners," a time-honored institution, which exists to this day. The farmers would meet on a certain day of the year and bid the number of rights they owned for certain pieces of salt hay. Sometimes, if the hay was located in the creek, you had to use a float to float it to the main-land. One had to get up early in the morning to cut it, while the dew was on it, for it was hard to cut. That salt hay now grows unmolested and no longer falls before the scythe of the mower.

"The Commoners" owned at one time miles of beach, but that has been sold for the most part. I remember that Teunis Bergen bought a half-mile of beach at Cedar Beach for $800, and "The Commoners" thought they had driven a big bargain. Mr. Bergen later sold this beach to Edwin H. Brown for $3,000.

Another thing that for many years has fallen into disuse is having oxen to work the fields. In fact, the only pair of oxen I ever saw working here was used by J. Alanson Overton, who lived on the road to Southold.

A boy, if he wanted to earn some extra money, was paid 50 cents for a long day's work of at least 12 hours.

Working Out Road Tax

We did not pay road-tax, as we do to-day. Cement and oiled roads were unheard of. The roads were sandy in summer and muddy in the spring. We worked out our road tax, in proportion to the assessment on our property. Most of the men would work just as conscientiously on the road as they would on the farm—I know my father did—but if the road overseer was not looking, the boys fell from pace. When we had a big snow-storm—and we had them those days, December being the worst month of the year—the road overseer would call out all hands to dig out the roads. There was fine sleighing then and everyone had a sleigh. Good sleighing would last for weeks. To the sweet music of the sleigh-bells, and well wrapped up in horse-blankets, the boys and girls, and older ones too, had a merry time. Sliding down hill and skating on the ponds were great sports.

J.B. Terry's Wharf

I well remember as a boy carting potatoes and turnips to J.B. Terry's Wharf at Town Harbor.[10] That was one of the busiest places in Southold. Mr. Terry had built a long wharf and hired a dredge to dredge out the sand at the end and side, so that the New York steamboats, under command of Capt. Geo. C. Gibbs and flying between Sag Harbor and New York, could land there. The first side-wheeler was the *W.W. Coit*, and later the *Montauk* and *Shelter Island* were put on the route. In the busy season the boats would make three trips a week. They would leave in the late afternoon and come in in the early morning.

Mr. Terry was a first-class business man and had a lumber and coal business and general store at the Harbor. He also shipped produce on commission. He later sold his coal business to George C. Terry. George Hahn was J.B. Terry's foreman, and a very capable one, too. The steamboats carried large cargoes of freight,[11] and also many passengers who enjoyed the sail to and from the city. Then, too, the fare was less than on the railroad. Stops were also made at Greenport, Shelter Island Heights and Orient, where hundreds of barrels of potatoes were taken on.

Charles M. Ledyard drove around the town and bought eggs of farmers' wives, and these eggs, together with farm produce, he would take on the boat to sell in New York. He would drive his faithful horse down to the wharf, and after he had left on the boat, the horse, minus a driver, would trot back home, where he was unharnessed and put in his stall. When it came time for Mr. Ledyard to return on the boat, the horse was put before the wagon, and he, as before without a driver, would trot down to the wharf to meet his master. There was a choice bit of poetry on the wagon, telling people not to stop the horse, and informing them "to let me goit, for I am going to meet my master on the Coit" (steamer *W.W. Coit*). Mr. Terry had a big horse by the name of Major. Major would be hitched to the large hand-car, loaded

J.B. TERRY'S WHARF, WITH THE STEAMER *W.W. COIT* APPROACHING
When Joseph Hallock was a boy, he carted farm produce to this wharf so that it could be shipped by steamer to New York City. Numerous passengers made the trip as well. The wharf was, wrote Joseph, "one of the busiest places in Southold." It was torn down in 1954.

with produce and would haul it down to the end of the wharf. After he was unhitched, he would jump off the wharf and swim ashore.

Mr. Terry sold his business at Town Harbor to Wm. A. Prince, and later became President of the Suffolk Co. Mutual Insurance Co. and President of the Southold Savings Bank, and was one of the most prominent citizens of the town. I little thought then that I would one day be one of his successors as President of the Bank. Mr. Terry thought very much of my father and was always a good friend to me. The wharf, and the land on which Mr. Terry's business buildings stood, now comprise the Town Harbor Village Park.

Camp Meetings

There were two camp-meetings in this vicinity, one at Shelter Island Heights (then Prospect) and the other at Jamesport, and I attended both as a boy. The Heights was started as a camp-meeting by some Brooklyn clergymen, and I can remember when there were only a few small, plain cottages there. Some of the greatest ministers in the country would preach, among them Dr. Storrs, Dr. Behrends, Methodist Bishops and others of like fame. This camp-meeting was interdenominational. The one at Jamesport was of the old-fashioned Methodist kind, and was largely attended by Methodists from all over the East End. We would start early and spend the whole day there. Sad to state, I fear I was more interested in the candy booth kept by Mr. Albertson, the candy man, than I was in the meetings, and I would sometimes walk down to the shore. This camp meeting was a Methodist institution for many years.

Aunt Esther and Aunt Jerusha

In a little old house, where is now the residence of Mr. Jones, just west of the Reydon Club golf grounds, lived "Aunt Esther" and "Aunt Jerusha." They were Hallocks and cousins of my father. They were very old, "Aunt Esther" being over 90. We would have them at our home for Thanksgiving and frequently on other days. I spent many Sunday afternoons with them at their home, always being treated to cookies, and was greatly entertained by their sprightly talk about old times. From "Aunt Esther," especially, I learned much of the history and traditions of the Hallock family. She had a prodigious memory and could remember events from the time she was four years old. To her mind, there was no question about the authenticity of Peter H. Hallock. Let me say here that the Hallock family owes a great debt to the late Lucius H. Hallock of Orient for his monumental history of the Hallocks.

Entertainment

We did not have the means of entertainment that our young people do to-day, and had far less time for it, and yet I question whether our present-day young people have any more, if as much, real enjoyment as did we. There were no movies, radios, automobiles or bicycles then. If one wanted to go to the village, which was seldom, we either had to hitch up the old horse, or, if the team had been working all day, had to walk, and we did not mind the walk at all. Many a time I have walked up to the village at night to attend the Good Templars' Lodge and then walked back home.

Our sports were swimming, which invariably began on Decoration Day, high-sky, pitching horse-shoes and base-ball. The latter game we played with a hand-made soft ball and one fired it at the runner when he was running to the bases. If we hit him, he was out. In the winter evenings, young and

A SIMPLER TIME
Children in Joseph Hallock's day had neither the "means" nor the "time" for
entertainment afforded "our young people…to-day." Here, two young women enjoy a ride
on an extremely rustic seesaw.

old men would meet around at the neighbors to play dominoes, and there
is where I learned to be a fair domino player.

There would always be plenty of apples and hard-cider and sometimes
the women-folks would have a batch of crullers or molasses cookies for
us. Dominoes and checkers were the great games. I could never master
the latter game, but my father and sister Lucy were excellent players. I
remember once when Lucy beat our next-door neighbor, "Uncle Moses"
Terry, he could hardly get over it, for he was a fine player. My mother was
a strict old-fashioned Methodist and would not allow a pack of cards in the
house. She also was greatly opposed to dancing, and in deference to her
wishes I never learned to dance. She changed greatly in her latter days, and
had no objection to my daughter dancing.

Three Red-Letter Days

The three great days of the year, in which we did no work, were Town Meeting Day, Fourth of July and Christmas.

Town Meeting

Town Meeting, which was held annually on the first Tuesday in April, met in the Presbyterian Church at Southold, and all the voters of Southold Town, from Franklinville (Laurel) to Orient, came there to vote and discuss Town affairs. If the election was likely to be pretty close, a few voters would come by sail-boat from Plum Island and Fisher's Island. The meeting was always opened with prayer by Rev. Dr. Epher Whitaker. I am afraid the young boys never heard the prayer or any of the proceedings of the Town Meeting.

The people voted by ballot. Neither the voting machines nor the Australian ballot, containing the names of all candidates, were known then. The ballots, instead of being prepared by the State, were printed by the two parties, Republican and Democratic. The ballots were small and contained only the names of the candidates of the one party. Sometimes a party candidate, generally the nominee for Tax Collector, which was the best paying office in the Town, would have his name printed on the opposition party ballot instead of the regular nominee. One had to look out for these split ballots. Pasters would also be used to paste over the name of the other candidate.

Where an appropriation of less than $500 was asked, the transfer of the dog tax to the general fund or on questions not involving the appropriation of money, the voters would vote by show of hands in "Open Town Meeting." Sometimes there would be hot discussions on matters at issue. There would be voted by ballot the appropriations for General Fund, Support of Poor and Board of Health.

REVEREND EPHER WHITAKER
Dr. Epher Whitaker, pastor of the Southold Presbyterian Church, played an active part in the community life of Joseph's childhood, speaking at fairs and celebrations and driving or walking every Wednesday evening to the Bay View School to give a religious talk there.

We had Local Option for and against the sale of liquor and beer by saloons, hotels and storekeepers. There was great interest in this question, and the temperance people, for weeks before election, would have speakers in the different villages to urge their hearers to vote No-License. Before Local Option, there were three Excise Commissioners, elected for three years each. At every Town Meeting before Local Option went into effect, an Excise Commissioner was voted for on a separate ballot, one candidate in favor of license and the other opposed. As a general thing, the license candidate won. I only voted in favor of license once, though I was not a teetotaler, and that was when the Prohibition party nominated a candidate against the Republican nominee for Supervisor, Jesse G. Case, who was a very strong temperance man. The Prohibition party should have endorsed Mr. Case, for Henry H. Reeve, the Democratic candidate, though he never drank himself, always advocated very strongly the licensing of the liquor traffic. That year I was so disgusted with Prohibition that I voted for license.

With the exception of Tax Collector, who was paid by a one-cent commission on every dollar collected within 30 days, and five cents thereafter, the fees of the town officials were very small, seldom being over $100 per year, and in many cases much less. There were no salaries paid. You received payment in fees. I remember that when I was first elected Town Clerk, some thirty years ago, all my fees amounted to only about $200 a year. I then only received $2.00 a day for Town Board meetings. With the issuing of marriage, dog and hunting licenses and the great increase in Town business, my fees amounted to $1,800 before I retired as Town Clerk, some four years ago, after 25 years of service in that office.

The older ones would meet friends they had perhaps not seen for a year, but the great attraction for the boys were the tables outside on which were arranged, in tempting display, candies, dates, oranges, crullers, cookies and pies. In company with other boys from Hog Neck, I started on foot, soon after sunrise, for the Mecca, to which we had been looking forward all the year. For months I had been saving my pennies for this event and generally had 50 cents to spend. There was not a cent left when I walked home at night. The Methodist ladies would always provide a big chicken-pie dinner for 50 cents for all who wished to buy, but for the most part people would bring their dinner with them. We boys, of course, could eat no dinner, even if we had the price to pay for it, for we had been gorging ourselves with the sweetmeats sold by the vendors. The Methodist church basement was kept open in the evening, and the Supervisor, Town Clerk and Justices of the Peace would eat supper there before counting the votes, which lasted until 2 o'clock the next morning. The Methodist ladies would have cakes, pies, fruit and candy for sale in the evening, and end up with an auction of the food left over. The boys would always be on hand, and if we were fortunate enough to have any money left after the day's orgy would proceed to promptly spend it. We forgot all the teachings we had received on the value of thrift on that day. For one day in the year we were reckless with our money.

There was always a hotly contested ball game in the afternoon. The Town would generally go Democratic, and Henry A. Reeves would be re-elected Supervisor year after year, and he would take practically the whole Democratic ticket with him, though occasionally a lone Republican would slip in by a few votes. Voters voted straight in those days. The two ends of the Town were strongly Republican, but the voters would come by horse and wagon, and many failed to come, especially if it was not a pleasant day. Greenport, the home of Henry A. Reeves, was overwhelmingly Democratic. The voters there would hire a special train, as most of the people had no horses. There would be four or five cars filled with Democrats and only one car of lone Republicans.

One reason that the Democrats were generally successful was that the Prohibition party ran a Town ticket. This party only pulled about one hundred voters, but as nine-tenths were former Republicans, a great part coming from the Republican stronghold of Orient, their strength was great enough, especially in a close election, to insure the election of the Democratic candidates. In this village there were only four or five Prohibitionists. In one national election, 1884, the Prohibition candidate for President, John P. St. John, pulled enough votes in New York State to insure the election of Grover Cleveland and the defeat of James G. Blaine, the Republican nominee. I was a great Blaine man and deeply mourned his defeat. But in later years, as I am to-day, I became a great admirer of Grover Cleveland and consider him one of our greatest Presidents.

In 1894 the Town voted at Town Meeting in election districts, and the old New England Town Meeting was a thing of the past. It had been one of the most cherished institutions of the Town since its founding. It was a great day. Friend met friend and exchanged greetings. Affairs of the Town were discussed in open Town Meeting and voted on. But as the population of the Town increased, it became almost impossible for all the voters to vote in one place. Voters would have to stand in line for two hours, and many, especially the older ones, would become disgusted and leave the line and go home. When the voters voted in election districts, Henry A. Reeves and the Democratic candidates were defeated by Dr. Barton D. Skinner and his Republican colleagues, and the Town has been in the Republican column for the most part ever since, with the exception that Supervisors Frank Tuthill and David W. Tuthill, Democrats, were elected for some years.

I well remember as a boy when I received my first political money, and by the way that was the only time I ever received money for working for my party candidates. Franklin H. Overton of Peconic was the Republican candidate for Supervisor in the old Town Meeting days. He gave me $2.00 (I thought it was a princely sum) to work for him among the votes of Hog Neck. Mr. Overton was elected by a very few votes, but I do not take credit for his election, even if I did my best to earn that $2.00.

I well remember one Town Meeting that I missed going to. The girl who worked for my mother had the measles, and to my great disgust I caught them from her just before Town Meeting. I called down all kinds of maledictions on that poor girl's head. At any other time I would not have cared so much. The only time I ever failed in voting was at the Town Meeting election in 1889. I had just come from Patchogue, where I had lived the past year, and not being 30 days in the election district, I was disfranchised.

—m—

Fourth of July

Fourth of July was the next great day in the calendar. As at Town Meeting, I zealously saved my money until I had acquired 50 cents, with which to purchase small firecrackers and torpedoes. Thank goodness there were no giant firecrackers going off with the noise of a bomb in those days! I would dispose of my supply in the morning. Then I was ready to go to the huge picnic at Paradise Point, which was participated in by the residents of Hog Neck, both young and old, male and female.

There was an immense clam-bake, bread, biscuit, pies, cakes, puddings and topping off with home-made ice cream, which it took about two hours to freeze. It was a Gargantuan feast! In the evening, the young folks would go up to Brushes Hill, where we could see the fireworks, and play games. I will confess that kissing games were the favorites, especially by the boys. And this held true for the surprise and other parties held at the young people's homes in the winter evenings. We would have thought it wicked to dance, and we did not know how.

Christmas

Christmas was the last great day of the year. In company with my brother and sisters, I would hang up my stocking and anxiously await the time for getting up. The first thing I would generally find in the top of the stocking would be a potato or turnip. Then would come in succession a nice red apple grown in our orchard, home-made molasses candy, a pair of mittens made by my mother, some nuts, a few sticks of store-candy, an orange, home made pop-corn, a stone or piece of coal and then, at the very bottom, a bought present—either a jackknife, baseball or, at one side, a pair of skates or a sled. I remember one year my father made me a large sled, and that outlasted any bought sled I ever had. We invariably never received but one bought present.

The girls would generally receive dolls, and if one would open its eyes and cry, it was considered among the seven wonders of the world. Who will say that we were not just as happy and appreciative of the small gifts we received as are the young people of today, with their wealth of gifts?

Thanksgiving

Thanksgiving and New Years were celebrated, but they could not compare with the three great days just mentioned. Turkey is now the chief dish for the Thanksgiving table, but in the old days it was an uncommon thing to have that bird as the piece-de-resistance. Turkeys were for the rich. My father could have afforded a turkey, but it was contrary to all his ideas of thrift, which he had been taught from his infancy, to pay out good money for something to eat when he had on hand meat or fowl.

Chickens were no treat, as we could kill a pair any time. However, we did often have a couple of roast roosters. A frequent dish was roast sparerib with all the meat on it. For a tasty morsel you can't beat it. Pigs' liver was also highly prized. We did occasionally have a goose. The table was bountifully supplied with vegetables and apple, mince and pumpkin pie. It was a feast all right.

New Years

We would always hang up our stockings on New Year's Eve, and would find in them home-made molasses candy, pop-corn, an apple, some bought stick-candy and an orange, but no bought present. We had an especially big dinner.

Religious Life

Now, as to my religious life. My mother was a staunch Methodist, brought up in that faith by my grandfather, Halsey Dickinson, who for many years was a class-teacher and led the weekly class at Bay View. He was one of the most gifted men in prayer and exhortation I ever heard. I well remember him and the class which I attended, and I would always give my testimony. My father was one of the best and noblest men I ever knew and I revere his memory, but he never attended a class-meeting and I never knew him to go to church. I never knew the reason why, but he was brought up in the stern Calvinistic Presbyterian faith by his father and grandfather, and I suspect that he, like many others, rebelled and made up his mind that when he became his own master he would live his own life, regardless of religious restrictions. My father may not have been outwardly religious, but he lived a strictly moral life.

Grandfather Dickinson regularly read the Bible through from cover to cover once a year, and he could repeat whole chapters verbatim. I never knew him to get stuck on where a certain passage could be found. The only secular reading he ever read was the Semi-Weekly *Evening Post*, which had been taken in our family ever since it was started, and the *Youth's Companion*. This paper was read by every member of the family, and I still continue to believe it was the finest youth's paper ever published. My mother read every word in it as long as she lived.

At an early age I began to go to the Methodist Church and Sunday School. The Sunday School was held in the basement of the church, as were the weekly prayer-meetings and special revival services held every winter. I always took a penny to drop in the church collection box, and also a penny for the Sunday School. On Missionary Sunday I would drop in either a five or ten cent piece. There was great rivalry between the Sunday School classes as to which would contribute the largest amount to Missions. My Sunday School teacher was Eli W. Howell, father of Mrs. Gilbert H. Terry.

I greatly prized taking out books from the Sunday School Library. My favorite author was E.P. Roe, though the Rollo books were not too far behind. The books in the Library were not of high literary value, but they taught clean living and right thinking.

The residents of Bay View did not go up to Southold to attend church Sunday evenings. Instead, a prayer meeting was held in the school house. There would be a different leader each evening. One by one, one would give his testimony and pray. The Moody and Sankey hymn book was used, and I loved to join in the singing. While I make no attempt to sing now, I still greatly enjoy hearing those old Gospel songs. Every Wednesday evening Rev. Dr. Epher Whitaker would either walk or drive down to the school house and give a religious talk, and I went out to hear him. Sometimes revival services would be held in the school house and last for weeks.

Circus and Play-Acting

One day, when I was a very small boy, the circus came to Greenport and my father took my brother Ben "to see the animals." I was told that I was too young to go. I felt pretty rare and went down to my step-grandmother's to tell her of my woes. She was a very strict Methodist, and soon convinced me of the awful sin of attending a circus.

BELMONT HALL, 1898
Belmont Hall, on Main Road opposite today's library, was the scene of many local cultural activities, including the plays in which Joseph Hallock was a frequent participant. In 1954, it was razed for a parking lot.

She had been reading Bunyan's *Pilgrim's Progress* to me, and I was greatly intrigued with the story. I asked to be dressed up as a Christian, and armed with a long stick, and having a paper-cap on my head and a shawl around me, I marched around switching the heads of weeds with my "sword." In imagination I was either slaying the devil or killing the animals in the circus. At another time my father took my brother to a Lyceum play at the Universalist Church (it not being used for church services then), and I was again kept at home on account of my youth. My only relief was in convincing myself that, like the circus, a play was a sink of iniquity. Little did I think then that acting on the stage of Belmont Hall would be one of my greatest joys, without a qualm of conscience.

Musical Career

My father bought a small melodeon of D.P. Horton, and my mother thought I should be taught music lessons. So Metta Horton was engaged to start the future musical genius on his career, and she came to our home once a week. The notes were all Greek to me, and so they remained. I was blessed with a pretty good memory, and while the teacher was playing, I would carefully watch, not the notes, but where she placed her fingers on the keys, and so I was able to play a few simple tunes. Miss Horton, with much disgust, said I had no musical talent, and I quite agreed with her. Later, when my sister became old enough to take music lessons, the melodeon was traded for an Estey organ, and then we had good music in the home, for the girls had no trouble in mastering the art.

Spiritualistic Séance

Mr. Benjamin Horton of Bay View was a Spiritualist, and a Mrs. Gardiner of Southold was a medium. Frequently, séances were held at the home of Mr. Horton. One night, in company with Jesse Terry, I went to a séance at Mr. Horton's. Mrs. Gardiner was there, and after the room was darkened, she went into a trance. The people were asked if they wished to ask any questions of the Indian maiden who was in communication with the medium. A Presidential campaign was on then, and I was greatly interested to learn if the Republican candidate, U.S. Grant, would be elected over Horace Greeley. So I boldly put that query. I was curtly answered that questions of mundane affairs were never answered, so I had to wait until the day after election to learn the result. That was the only time I ever attended a séance.

No Black Hens

For the most part, the voters of Bay View were Republicans. They were of the old stock, and there were only six families of foreign birth there, four Irish and two German. A native of Poland had never been seen. One of the old residents, Alfred Wells, one of the finest men who ever lived, was such a rank Democrat that he would not have a black hen on his place. The Republicans were known as Black Republicans because they had favored the freeing of the slaves. Mr. Wells, or "Uncle Alfred," as he was called, took great pride in keeping his fields clean, and you would never see a weed on his farm. Nearly every one of the old residents was either called "Uncle" or "Aunt," though they were of no relation.

First Physician

The first physician I remember was Dr. Van Water. Dr. Ireland of Greenport was sometimes called in consultation. Dr. Van Water was a first-class, all-round family doctor and was worshipped by all his patients, and they comprised all the residents within many miles. Next to one's family, he was the most dearly loved man in town. He was a bachelor and lived at Wm. Wells' hotel, which stood where the Savings Bank now stands. I remember as a small boy going with my father and mother to Dr. Van Water's funeral in the Presbyterian Church. The church was packed with mourners, many being unable to get inside, but all waited to file by the casket containing the earthly remains of their beloved doctor. Ian Maclaren never portrayed a finer doctor of the old school

Dr. Hartranft's House, Main Road
An impressive residence, everyone knew where Dr. Hartranft lived. His home (and office) were located on the corner of Main Road and Youngs Avenue.

Dr. Van Water was succeeded by Dr. A.L. Sweet, and he by our beloved Dr. Hartranft, whom we all so well knew and who ranked as one of the most skillful physicians on Long Island.

The Good Neighbor

There were no trained nurses in those days, and when one was quite sick it was the custom for the neighbors to come at night and take turns in sitting up with the sick one, so that the tired-out family could have some rest. Many a night have I sat up with an ill neighbor and given him his medicine at a certain hour. A great repast of meat-sandwiches, mince-pie, cake and <u>strong</u> coffee was provided for the watchers. And after they had drank that coffee, there was no trouble in keeping awake. If one of the men-folks was sick, the neighbors would all turn out and do his farm-work free of charge. "The Good Neighbor" was a concrete fact in those days.

The Southold Butcher

In the summer-time, after we had eaten up all our fresh meat, Hezekiah Jennings, the Southold butcher, would drive down to Bay View once a week, and my mother would go out to the wagon when Mr. Jennings rang his big bell in front of our house and buy two pounds of round steak. It would have been beneath Mr. Jennings' dignity to get out of the wagon and come to the door to inquire if we wanted anything. The steak was from home-beef, cut from cows too old to milk, and gracious, wasn't it tough! But we had good teeth and strong stomachs, and that steak was a welcome change once a week from the salt pork on which we had been feasting.

Speaking of salt-pork makes me think of a dish my mother often made—salt-pork, fried crisp, with milk-gravy. That, dished with boiled potatoes, made a feast fit for the gods. I still love it.

County Fair

The first County Fair I ever attended was at Greenport. I was so young that my recollection of it is very hazy. It was held on the lot where is now the ball-ground. Later, a Town Fair was held at Oak Lawn, and I had great fun

RIVERHEAD FAIRGROUNDS
Fences hold back the crowds at the Riverhead Fairgrounds. Young Joseph Hallock attended the annual county fair by train, returning "more tired when I got home than if I had worked in the fields all day."

attending it. There was a half-mile race-track there, and there was great excitement over the local horses which would compete for the $25.00 purse. I remember that my father took some wheat to the Fair to compete for the 50 cts. Prize, and I was greatly disappointed that he did not receive the blue-ribbon.

Later I went to the County Fair at Riverhead each year. I would go up on the early morning train and stay all day, and ride home on the evening train. Riverhead was too long a journey to go to by horse and wagon. The LIRR would run several special trains, as well as the regular ones, and they were all crowded. I had great sport seeing the sights, visiting with friends and relations and spending what little money I had left after paying my car-fare and admission on candy and peanuts and pop-corn. I was more tired when I got home than if I had worked in the fields all day.

Harvest Home

D. Philander Horton was the moving spirit in the Harvest Home Festivals, which were held each August at Oak Lawn. That was a great day. I always joined the thousands from all parts of the Town, as well as many from neighboring towns. Under the direction of Prof. Horton, patriotic songs were sung. Dr. Epher Whitaker always offered the opening prayer. Speeches were made by Nat. W. Foster, George F. Stackpole and Judge James H. Tuthill of Riverhead, Judge Henry P. Hedges of Bridgehampton, Rev. William F. Whitaker, a rising young preacher who even then gave evidence of his later great ability as a pulpit orator, and others.[12]

There would be a parade, led by Charles Floyd Smith on a charger. At first music was furnished by the Peconic Fife and Drum Corps and later by the Southold Brass Band. G. Frank Hommel would make great kettles of clam chowder, which was sold by the Ladies' Monumental Union, and if the kettle was likely to run dry, he would add sufficient water so that the crowd would not go away hungry. It was always well to buy your chowder early.

THE SOUTHOLD CORNET BAND, CIRCA 1900
The Southold Cornet Band was founded before 1882 and so would have participated in
both anniversary celebrations recalled by Joseph Hallock. It also took part in the town's
annual Harvest Home Festivals. (Joseph calls them the "Southold Brass Band.")

Bicycling

With the advent of the safety-bicycle, bicycling came into great favor, and
nearly everyone rode a bicycle. My wife, my sister and I each had one, and
"Little Ann" had her small wheel. We had great sport riding, and often
took trips as far as Mattituck. Bicycle paths were made along side of the
roads, and there would be a big cavalcade, led by Chas. Floyd Smith. Who
will question that the bicycle was not more conducive to health than the
automobile?

Tallow-Candle Days

I can go back in memory to the time when I would see my mother pouring the melted tallow into the candle-moulds, and I would often read by the tallow-candle. When it was time to go to bed, I would take my candle and march up-stairs to my cold, unheated room. Many a time I have seen my breath freeze in the zero atmosphere while lying in bed. Instead of a warming-pan, used in earlier generations, I would take up to bed either a hot hickory stick, about 14 inches long, or a hot brick, wrapped up in a woolen cloth. This I would first put in the center of the bed to get it warm, and when I was undressed would put it at the foot to keep my feet warm. By the aid of this bed-warmer and plenty of heavy woolen bedclothes, I could keep warm. What would the youth of to-day think of these hardships? We thought nothing of them—took them as a matter of course. And we grew up strong, hardy men and women, ready to cope with the world.

To save matches, which cost good money, we would wind paper-lighters and would always have a jar full on the mantelpiece.

Experience with Horses

I was never much of a horseman and was afraid of a horse if it had any life in it—and the horse, with uncanny wisdom, knew it. If I ever hired a livery-horse, which was seldom, I would always demand as the first requisite that it should be gentle. I well remember one day when Frank and Minnie

Smith[13] and Ella and I took a steamboat ride to Sag Harbor and there hired a horse to take us to East Hampton. As usual, I called for a gentle horse. That livery-stable keeper told no lie when he said that particular horse was gentle. It was not only gentle, but lazy, and we had an awful time getting to our destination and had to cut our visit short in order to allow time to meet our boat. Frank declared that the next time he would hire the horse, even if it ran away with us.

Perhaps my fear of a horse is owing to an incident that happened when I was a small boy. We had a very large and powerful horse named Jim. Jim had one fault, and that was that he would run away every chance he got. One day my Uncle Nelson was loading the wagon with a harrow and plow, preparatory to going down lot. A boy friend, Gilbert Terry, and myself were in the wagon. The horse-lines were on the ground, and quick as a flash Jim started to run. We had a perilous ride. The plow went out, followed by the big harrow, then one by one every board in the wagon except the board we were sitting on. I said to Gilbert, "I guess we better jump now," and jump we did, and aside from a few minor bruises were unhurt. It is a miracle that when the harrow fell out we were not caught in its teeth and seriously injured.

I remember another experience with a horse, or rather horses. When I worked for Mr. Van Dusen[14] in the Traveler office, I thought it was too far to walk the six miles there and back to my home. So I purchased a beautiful little pony for $100. I also bought a high, second-hand sulky. Perched on it I must have presented a ludicrous sight, for the sulky was much higher than the pony. The pony had never been broken properly, and I was the last one who should have undertaken the job. It had nothing to do except carry me back and forth from business, and it felt pretty good. It was too much for me and I sold it for $90, and with proper training it soon became a "ladies' horse."

I then went up to see Jake Brown, a horse-trader. He showed me a black team, either of which he would sell for $125. He said I could take one home and try it, and if I was not satisfied I could bring it back and he would give me the other. I found my horse stumbled, and as I did not want it to break its neck, I took it back and got the other. That horse had not one, but two, faults. It would "shy," and if it got the reins under its tail, it would hug them, so it was impossible to get them loose unless you hung over the dashboard and pulled them out. One day, riding down the steep side of Brushes Hill, the lines got caught under the horse's tail, and before I could free them, the sulky went over into the deep ditch and I pitched out head-first and landed on my shoulder, so that I was unable to go to work for several days. The horse was caught by a neighbor.

FRANK SMITH

Frank Smith, the milliner of Peconic, and his wife, Minnie, were close friends of Joseph and Ella Hallock and shared many of their activities. They were part of the "Two Days' Sails," and took part in a humorously slow horse-and-buggy ride as described in this memoir.

I sent word to Mr. Brown to come and get that devil of a horse, for I would not drive it again, and bring a gentle horse to trade for it. He brought a large, beautiful, gentle horse, but unfortunately it had the heaves. I had to pay $25 to boot. However, it had the prime essential of being gentle, and I kept it until I moved to Patchogue, when Mr. Brown came and took it and later sold it for $75. I then and there concluded that I was not cut out for a horse-trader, and I have never owned a horse since. In a short time I had lost over $100.

—m—

250th Anniversary Celebration

The greatest day that Southold had ever seen was the 250th Anniversary Celebration of Southold Town on August 27, 1890. Dr. Epher Whitaker was the moving spirit in the affair. Thousands were present from all parts of Southold Town and Suffolk County, and there were many visitors from beyond their borders. There was an immense parade, led by Alvah M. Salmon as grand marshal. Peter Gaffga drove four oxen before a venerable ox-cart. The Peconic Fife and Drum Corps played. There were brass bands from all parts of the Town and Shelter Island; a company on bicycles; an Indian canoe mounted on wheels; a cabriolet containing a lady and gentleman in the costumes of 1776, representing George and Martha Washington, with a negro coachman; a cavalcade of citizens on their own steeds; large farm wagons profusely decorated with flowers, and filled with women and young girls all dressed in white, representing the different villages in the Town; the Southold Fire Department, in which I marched; and then a train of 500 carriages, representing every style of make and decoration.

The morning session was held in the Presbyterian Church, that being the church founded in 1640. Dr. Whitaker gave words of welcome; prayer was offered by Rev. B.J. Abbott of the Methodist Church; Rev. J.H. Ballou of the Universalist Church read from Barnabas Horton's Family Bible; patriotic songs under the direction of Prof. D.P. Horton were sung; and

Rev. Dr. Richard S. Storrs, one of the foremost pulpit orators of the day, gave the oration.

The afternoon session was held at Oak Lawn. Hon. James H. Tuthill of Riverhead (that town being originally a part of Southold Town) presided. There was plenty of music under the direction of Prof. Horton, and addresses were made by Nat W. Foster, Rev. Wm. F. Whitaker, Wilmut M. Smith and Judge Henry P. Hedges. The evening meeting was held in the Presbyterian Church, and was presided over by Supervisor Henry A. Reeves. Prayer was offered by Rev. Wm. H. Littell. The address of the evening was made by Charles B. Moore of New York City, author of *Personal Indexes of Southold Town*. As a result of the Celebration, the Founders' Monument was erected in the Presbyterian Cemetery, on the site of the first Meeting House.

Twenty-five years later, in July 1915, an even greater celebration was held here to commemorate the 275th Anniversary of the Town. Now gaily decorated automobiles, instead of wagons and carriages, were in the immense parade, but Peter Gaffga drove a yoke of oxen, hitched to the same ox-cart he used in 1890. The celebration lasted for several days, a colorful and finely written account of which appears in Ella B. Hallock's "Story of the 275th Anniversary Celebration of the Founding of Southold Town." Ann drove a finely decorated Vassar car in the parade, and well remembers it.

The time draws near, 1940, when the Town will celebrate its 300th Anniversary.

The New School Teacher

One winter, when I was 20 years old, a bright, beautiful young school teacher, Ella Boldry, came from the Albany Normal School to teach the Bay View district school. It was always thought that we had to have a man teacher in the winter in order to handle the big boys, but my father, who was Trustee, thought he would risk hiring a young lady, especially as this particular young lady came highly recommended by Dr. Alden, the President of the Albany Normal, as a very fine teacher and an excellent disciplinarian. She lived up to her reputation, and had no trouble with any of the scholars. She was the best teacher the school ever had. She staid only one winter, as she secured a much finer position up-State, and during the next eight years held numerous responsible places, serving one year as Associate Editor of the *New York School Journal*. She was a born teacher, and a very successful one.

I well remember the first time I met the new teacher. She was to board at our home, and I drove up to the evening train to meet her. It was a bitterly cold night, and I was in an open schooner-wagon. After I had put her trunk in the wagon, I wrapped her up in the horse blankets and we proceeded on our three-mile journey home. On the way home, she asked me if I was the Trustee of the school. "No," I replied, "my father is the Trustee. I am only a boy." She told me afterwards that her heart went down when I made that statement, for knowing that she was to live in our home, she thought I would be pestering her with my attentions, and perhaps try to make love to her. Well, as a matter of course, I did immediately fall for her, and, wonder of wonders, she soon reciprocated my love, and before she left we became engaged.

It was not until eight years after that the love was consummated in marriage. I would go up to her home at Green Island, N.Y., occasionally during her vacations, not more often than once a year, and sometimes longer than that, and once or twice she came down to spend a few days with us. We carried on a steady correspondence, and I eagerly awaited her weekly letters. She told me the thing that attracted me to her more than anything else was the fact that I was a great reader of standard works, especially biography and history, and that I could discuss pretty well current and former events. She thought I had brains.

It is strange how some things will stand out in your memory. In shooting at a mark on New Year's Day, my father won a turkey. We had it for dinner the next day, and we thought how the new teacher would appreciate the feast! We helped her bountifully to the white and dark meat. We also had eels, and my mother asked Miss Boldry if she would like to try some. Coming from a fresh-water country, she had never seen or tasted eels before. On tasting them, she asked my mother if she minded if she put back the turkey and had an extra helping of eels. I gaped in astonishment. I could not understand it. Eels were a common dish in our home. You could go and catch them any time, but turkey was a dish fit for the gods, had as a general thing only on Thanksgiving. Eels remained a favorite dish of my wife all her life, and she dearly loved all kinds of sea-food.

"THE NEW SCHOOL TEACHER"
Joseph Hallock and Ella Boldry met in 1881, when she came to Southold to teach at the
Bay View School for the year and roomed with the Hallocks. They became engaged that
year, but it would be eight years before they married.

Ella and I spent many happy days together that first winter. We would go skating (she was a wonderful skater), take rides Sunday evenings—generally to the Cutchogue Methodist Church to hear Rev. David Macmullen—went to parties and on sleigh-rides. Under my tutorship, Ella became a fine domino player. For the last two or three years of our 45 years together, we always played a few games of backgammon in the evening. We also had a parlor pool-table, and she became quite expert in that game.

To return to the first winter—the term at school ended all too soon, and I was very downcast after Ella went away, but we both looked forward to a happy future together. To my youthful mind, when she taught our district school—and the same feeling has continued to this day, when my hair is grey with age and her presence is only a cherished memory—the new teacher, Ella Boldrey, was the most beautiful girl and woman, in features, mind and character, I ever met. Memories are precious, and I live in them.

Matrimonial Bureau

It was said that the Bay View school was a matrimonial bureau for young lady teachers. Jane Halsey married Gilbert W. Horton; Mary Wells married Charles E. Terry; Mary Curtis married George Henry Terry; Carrie Huntting married Jesse Terry; Ida Leslie married Ezra G. Beebe; and Ella Boldry married me. Other young lady teachers later married men from away. My uncle, J. Nelson Dickinson, married one of his scholars, Mary L. Young.

The Old School House

Some years ago the old school house was closed, and a neat two-room school house was built farther north on Jacob's Lane. There the children could not look out of the windows of the house at the forks of three roads at all who passed by, as in the old house. The latter school is now closed and the children are taken by bus to the fine High School at Southold. We trust the original school house, which is now the property of Miss Mary L. Dayton, will never be torn down but will continue to stand, to revive pleasant memories to the older ones and to show the young folks where their grandfathers and grandmothers attended school.

I Learn the Printer's Trade

I became very tired of farming. While there was a living in it then, there was not much money left after expenses had been paid. My love for Ella spurred on my ambition, and at the age of 21 I went to Greenport to learn the printer's trade of L.F. Terry in the Suffolk Times office. I staid there one year, and then Trustee Wm. H. Beebe of the Bay View school, which I had attended as a boy, offered me the position of teacher at $8.00 per week. That seemed pretty good money then, especially as I could board at home, and I accepted. I taught one year, and that was enough for me, though I got along all right with my scholars. I concluded I was not made for the teaching profession.

Fortunately, at that time Mr. B. Van Dusen offered me the position of associate editor of the *Long Island Traveler*, at $8.00 per week. I liked the work and think I had some aptitude for it, and I continued in country newspaper work for 45 years, until July 1927. I was associate editor of the *Patchogue Advance* for one year, and in April 1889, I returned to Southold and purchased the *Long Island Traveler*, and the editing and publishing of it became my life-work.

THE *LONG ISLAND TRAVELER* OFFICE, CIRCA 1895
Joseph Hallock bought the *Traveler* in 1889 and ran it until 1927. The second floor of the
office building (on Traveler Street, just south of the railroad tracks) was also his first home
as a married man, and his daughter Ann was born there. Here he is shown posing in front
of the office, with his foreman, Lew Wilkinson, to his right and his sister, Lucy, to his left.
Beside her, his wife Ella stands, holding a bicycle.

Our Honeymoon

On May 28, 1889, my sweetheart, Ella Boldry, and I were married at her
home on Green Island, N.Y. We left on the train for New York, and staid
all night at the Grand Union Hotel (now torn down), right across from
the Grand Central R.R. The next day we came home on the evening
train. That was our honeymoon trip. Seven years later we spent a week in
Washington, and called that our wedding trip.

THEODORE SHIPHERD
"Ted" Shipherd, Joseph's first printer's devil at the *Long Island Traveler*, later became a
Congregational minister. He said he "owed much" to his training there.

When I was married I had neither time nor money for a wedding trip.
Two days after I was married I was hard at work sticking type in the *Traveler*
office. When I took charge of the *Traveler* office, Justice (not [yet] Justice)
Herbert M. Hawkins was the foreman, and a very capable one, too, and

Lewis P. Wilkinson was a type-setter. They had both worked with me when I was employed by Mr. Van Dusen. Herbert told me I should have a printer's devil,[15] so I engaged Theodore (Ted) M. Shipherd and he staid with me for three years. He afterwards was graduated from Williams College, and is now a Doctor of Divinity and pastor of a big Congregational church at Norwalk, Conn.

When Theodore left to attend college, his brother, H. Robinson (Rob) Shipherd, came in as printer's devil. He became a very fine job printer. After a few years, he, like his brother, entered and graduated at Williams College and took post-graduate work at Harvard, where he attained his degree of Doctor of Philosophy. He then became a professor at Harvard and later at Boston University, and still later became President of different Western colleges. He is now pastor of a Congregational church in Iowa. Both of the Shipherd boys pay me the compliment of saying they owe much to their training in the old *Traveler* office.

After a few years, Herbert went to Greenport and became foreman of the *Suffolk Times* office. Later, he and Samuel L. Bennett purchased the *Greenport Watchman*, which they ran for some time. Herbert is now a successful businessman, and for some time has been a valued member of the Southold Town Board, as Justice of the Peace. When Herbert left my employ, Lewis P. Wilkinson became the foreman, and he has continued in that capacity to this day. He is a first-class, all-round printer. He is very conscientious in his work, and he had my full confidence the many years he worked for me.

Lewis was very fond of my mother, and she was of him, and nearly every Sunday he would spend an hour with her in her room. She always looked forward to his visits. He said those visits did him more good than if he had gone to church.

Other boys that I employed for a time were William A. Richmond, Mortimer Jewell, Joseph (Horace Greeley) Wells, Lewis P. Wilkinson Jr. (now manager of the Bohack store), Wilson Glover, Clifford Prince and Clarence Conklin, still employed in the office.

Our First Home

Ella and I made our first home in the little rooms over the *Traveler* office, and there we spent some of the happiest days of our lives. There our daughter Ann was born, and to the fond parents she was the most wonderful baby who ever lived. She was the same to her grandmothers Hallock and Boldry and to her Aunts Lucy and Grace.

This page and previous:
ANN AND HER
GRANDMOTHERS
Ann "could do no wrong" in
the eyes of her grandmothers,
according to her father. Here
she is on the Maple Lane porch
with Grandmother Maria
Jane (Dickinson) Hallock and
Grandmother Ann Boldry, her
namesake (opposite).

Writer and Lecturer

My wife was of great aid to me in the editorial work of the *Traveler*, as
she possessed a very fine and polished style in composition and could tell
a story most graphically. For a time after our marriage, Ella was Assistant
Principal of Southold Academy under Mrs. Louise Pond Jewell. Later she
attained much fame as lecturer on physiology and hygiene before Teachers'
Institutes in Massachusetts, New York, and Pennsylvania, under the auspices
of the State Departments of Education of those states. She was a valued
correspondent of several metropolitan papers and magazines. She was the

author of a number of books, among them *Translation of Grimm's Fairy Tales*, *In Those Days* (her favorite), *Introduction to Browning* (of which she was a great student and teacher), *Some Living Things*, *Lessons on the Human Body*, *Story of King Arthur*, *William Tell*, *Cabin Paradise* and *History of the 275th Anniversary of Southold Town*.

After Ella's death, her daughter Ann had published as a memorial volume *Robert Browning's Star and Glad Message*, the manuscripts of which had been prepared by her mother. Ella was truly a very talented and busy woman. And notwithstanding all her literary work, she was a first-class housekeeper and took wonderful care of her home.

—⚍—

Two Days' Sail

While Ella and I were both busy people, we took time to play. The "Two Days' Sail," held once a year, was a great event. A party of young people would charter a sloop and sail forth for Montauk, Three-Mile Harbor, New London or some other port, where we would spend the night. "The Harp," under command of Capt. Bill Maynard, was not a palatial yacht. Straw would be put in the hold, and with plenty of blankets, male and female being separated by the center-board, we attempted to sleep during the night. But there was little rest, for someone would complain of the hard bed and would prowl around and go up on deck to get some fresh air. Enough food would be taken to feed a multitude.

One day, in Fort Pond Bay,[16] a mighty wind came up and we were nearly shipwrecked. At another time the sloop ran on a sandbar off Sag Harbor and had to stay there until the tide rose. Addie Avery, who was with us, wanted to be taken ashore in the row-boat and said she would walk home. As the walk would have been about fifty miles, we persuaded her not to desert the ship.

I well remember the night we made harbor at New London wharf. It was an awful hot night, and Ella and I, rather than go down in the stuffy hold to sleep, took our blankets and slept on deck. A heavy thunder-storm came

Two Days' Sail, August 23–24, 1901

Joseph and Ella Hallock and their friends put a lot of youthful energy into their annual "Two Days' Sail" excursions, with overnights at nearby ports like Montauk or New London, where "enough food would be taken to feed a multitude." In 1901, Joseph's sister Lucy and friend Minnie Smith prepared a scrapbook, with captions and sketches, to commemorate the event. *Courtesy of the Southold Free Library.*

up and we were drenched to the skin. Using our blankets as umbrellas, we walked up to the railroad station, at 2 o'clock in the morning, and went in the waiting room. We were eyed most suspiciously as tramps or something worse, but after explaining to the officer our predicament and why we were there, he relented, decided not to take us to the lock-up to sober up after a drunk and took us down-stairs, so that we could dry ourselves by the furnace in the cellar. As we went down we saw a huge rat scamper by in fear of its life, and I didn't blame it, for we were a sight.

One day, on one of our trips, I was lucky enough to catch a bluefish in Plum Gut. This was the first and only bluefish I ever caught by hook and line. The poet of the party, Minnie Terry Smith, in lyric verse told, among other striking events of the two days' sail, how "Josie caught a blue." We all know what a master of finished prose Minnie is, but let me tell you that that poem was a masterpiece and should remain forever in the archives of the club. I remember one day when we had planned the two-days' sail, and the women-folks had prepared enough food to feed an army, a big storm came up and we decided to have our sail in Mrs. Bliss' large barn. This we did, slept in the hay-loft, ate up all the grub, told stories and played games.

—⁓—

Fishing Trips

AT THE END OF A MEN'S FISHING EXCURSION
Joseph Hallock describes men-only fishing trips off of Shelter Island in his youth. These unidentified gentlemen have been on such a trip, but their catch seems modest.

There were also the two-days' fishing trips for men only, with Lewis H. Tuthill as Commodore, the destination for the night generally being a cove on the far-side of Shelter Island. We would fish off Green Hill in the late afternoon and early morning for sea-bass, and would always catch enough for a delicious chowder, made by David Jackson, and enough fish to take home. I remember once I caught the largest fish and was very proud of my prowess. We slept either on deck in our blankets or in the straw in the hold. But there was very little sleep, for some were sure to be wakeful, and I was among that number, and they felt it their bounden duty to keep all the others awake. At sunrise we were off to the fishing grounds.

Six Days' Sail

A few times, quite a number of men would charter a schooner for a six-days' cruise. We would sail as far as Nantucket, making port at Block Island, Martha's Vineyard, Newport, New Bedford, Wood's Hole and New London. I remember one time we spent the night at Newport. Capt. Bill Maynard, who was nearly seven feet, and Ezra Tillinghast, a dwarf, about as wide as he was tall, led us in procession as we marched through the fashionable streets of the city. The residents looked on in wonder, especially at the leaders, but we were not arrested for disturbing the peace.

At other times we sailed west, and made port at New Haven, Bridgeport and other places along the Connecticut shore. As on the other trips, we would sleep on the straw in the hold. We would take plenty of provisions, and would replenish our stock at the different ports. These trips were good fun, at very little expense. At each port we would either walk around or get in a bus and take sight-seeing trips. Once we landed on the Long Island shore and took a railroad trip to Coney Island. It was my first visit there.

Good Times with Henry G. Howell

I loved to fish and would often go for a day's fishing off Shelter Island, my companion generally being Henry G. Howell. Speaking of Mr. Howell brings to mind the evenings I used to spend with him and some other cronies in the little back-room of his drug store. Samuel Dickerson, Ed Corey, Dick Sturges and Nick Carey were always sure to be there. Mr. Howell was a very bright man intellectually, and while we did not sit on flour-barrels around the old-time grocery store to decide the fate of the Nation, we did our best to do so as we sat in our chairs and watched the smoke curling up from our pipes.

I Join Orders and Engine Co.

While I was at Patchogue, I was raised to the sublime degree of Master Mason in South Side Lodge, F&AM,[17] and on my return to Southold, affiliated with Peconic Lodge of Greenport. I also joined Southold Lodge of Odd Fellows.

Protection Engine Co. had been organized here while I was at Patchogue, and when I returned I immediately became a member. I am now the oldest member, both in age and in years of service. With loving memory I recall those charter members—Howard Huntting, Richard S. Sturges, J. Edward Corey, William H. Terry, George C. Terry, Samuel L. Bennett, Oliver V. Penney, Abraham F. Lowerre—all my good friends. And how we used to enjoy those clam chowders.

We had what we now call a "dinkey engine," and it is still preserved as a relic in our modern firehouse, with its up-to-date equipment. This engine was of course manned by man-power, and I ran to many a fire. Some

FIRST FIRE ENGINE

As one of the first members of Southold's first fire department, Protection Engine Company, Joseph Hallock knew what it was like to pull its first engine, No. 1, by hand. "I ran to many a fire," he said.

PROTECTION ENGINE COMPANY, 1929

The members of Southold's Protection Engine Company, founded in 1886 (Hallock mistakenly says 1889 in his memoir), pose with their equipment. Joseph joined in 1889 and was the oldest living member when he wrote these memoirs.

years later a larger engine was purchased, and that was truly a man-killer. One soon got winded in pumping, and another would jump in to take your place.

On every Christmas morning we would have a firemen's parade, and would cheer ourselves hoarse as we received cakes, pies, fruit and cigars all along the line of march, from "The Run" to Town Harbor Lane.[18] We presented a gaudy appearance in our red shirts and helmet hats. As the firemen neared our house, Ann would always come out with a large cake, and the walkers would ring with "Three cheers for Ann Hallock," and her mother, grandmother and aunt were as proud as Yaphet[19] as they stood on the front porch.

I Become a Play-Actor

When Protection Engine Co.'s firehouse was built, there was a debt of $1,000 on it, and it was decided that the easiest way to pay it off was to give plays in Belmont Hall,[20] at which an admissions fee of 25 cents and 35 cents for reserved seats was to be charged. Southold has always had much dramatic talent, and there was no trouble in getting players to fill the caste. Acting on the stage was meat and drink to me, and I took part in every play. I preferred and usually took a comedy part. We would give two or three plays every winter.

Geo. M. Baker's plays were our favorite repertory. Old Belmont Hall would be packed for two nights, and as we had little expense, we were able to pay off the debt on the Engine House, and also raised $500 to buy a piano for the school, and had a nice sum in the treasury when we turned the money over to the Southold Players.

We not only played at Southold, but also at Greenport, Mattituck and Riverhead, and we were always greeted with big houses and achieved quite a reputation. When we played in other towns, we always had a big supper at the hotel, and that we charged to expenses. We thought the supper was due us, as that was the only remuneration we received. We

THE CAST OF *THE STOLEN WILL*, CIRCA 1935

Joseph Hallock (with whiskers, left of center, front row) played "Chip Winkle, Esq., a long, lank country boy" in this long-running production to raise money for the Protection Engine Company.

would furnish our own costumes, borrow the needed furniture, etc., and use the stage scenery in the hall. Perhaps the plays were not as artistically done as in later days, but we pleased the audience and had a nice net sum at the end of the season.

The play that had the greatest run, and in which I starred as "Chip Winkle, Esq., a long, lank country boy," was *The Stolen Will*. This play was presented three times, about ten years apart, at Southold, Greenport, Mattituck and Riverhead, each time being greeted with crowded houses. I continued to take the leading role of "Chip" at each performance, though most of the other members of the caste were changed each time. We netted over $900 from *The Stolen Will*. My special playing companion, as "Betsy Smith, a bold, bad woman," was, for the first two productions, Julia L. Conklin, and for the last time, Louise Goldsmith. Neither Mrs. Conklin nor myself could commit our lines verbatim. As for myself, I never said my lines twice the same way. We were of course careful to give the right cue at the end. Some way we were always able to pull ourselves out of a hole, and I never had to be prompted. In fact, the prompter would not have been able to do so, and I knew it, and also knew that I had to work out my own salvation.

I always learned my lines—that is, as well as I could—before the first rehearsal. Then I could give my whole attention to the acting. I had to take my own conception of the part, no trainer could teach it to me, and then I had to live the part and forget myself. "Chip Winkle," not Joe Hallock, was on the stage. As "Chip," I had to crawl under the sofa to hide from "Betsy," and I once became stuck there. It was a critical moment, but by a mighty effort I extricated myself, but not without tearing my shirt almost off my back. I remember that once Mrs. Conklin forgot her lines entirely and her mind was a blank. But, as always, she was equal to the emergency, and, as it was a farm scene, she pretended to be feeding the chickens, calling "chick, chick" as she went off to one side of the stage to get her lines from the prompter. Then she was all right.

Both Julia and Louise were superb comedy actresses, and I greatly enjoyed playing with them. My days for acting on the stage are over, but I shall ever recall, with the greatest of pleasure, the old days when I "strode across the boards," behind the glare of the footlights. I do not care much for movies, but I still dearly love to see a good play and fine acting.

—◊—

Cabin-Paradise

My wife dearly loved the woods and water, and, when Ann was a little girl, we decided to build a log-cabin on my mother's land at Paradise Point. The building and furnishings of this cabin are fully and beautifully described in the booklet, *Cabin-Paradise*, by Ella B. Hallock. With the exception of a summer clam-baking resort kept by Geo. W. Bullock at the far end of the Point, about half-a-mile distant, we had the only habitation there. We were the "first settlers." Quite a contrast to the beautiful resort it is to-day, the shore front being dotted with beautiful homes and studios. The original cabin was very crude, only one room, with no conveniences, but it had a big fireplace. Nevertheless, we spent many happy days there. Ella, Ann and I would ride on our bicycles, laden with provisions, through the four miles of sandy roads to the cabin. I would ride back and forth to my work at the *Traveler* office each morning and night, and the bicycle always brought a supply of eatables. We would spend a week at a time there.

We had a row-boat on the shore, and would go out for a row each afternoon when I arrived. Later, the cabin was enlarged by additions to the side and rear and we had sleeping quarters up-stairs, but we never had more fun than in the original one-room cabin, built out of logs by Capt. Bacon and Webb Gordon. In time, two other bungalows were built, one of which was removed to our "open lot" and is now "The Bandbox," with all conveniences. My wife received quite a revenue in renting out the bungalows. For full particulars of our happy summer vacations, read *Cabin-Paradise*.

The year before the cabin was built, Ella, Ann and I spent a week at the Crows' Fish House at Indian Neck,[21] which was put at our disposal by Henry D. and Met Horton. There we had not beds or cots to sleep on, but bunks, and we did our cooking by the huge fireplace. One night, the bunk seemed especially hard, and I took my blankets and slept outside on the sand. We had a wonderfully jolly week, and I think that then and there Ella made up her mind to build a cabin for ourselves at Paradise Point.

CABIN-PARADISE
When the Hallocks built their tiny retreat on Paradise Point at the turn of the century, they were the "first settlers." This photo shows the structure before a chimney was added. *Left to right*: Ann (in tree), Joseph and Ella (apparently sketching) enjoying nature.

Paradise Point

In the days long ago, before I can remember, there was a fish factory on the east side of the very tip of Paradise Point, owned and operated by Jake Appley. It burned down, and I remember seeing the ruins.

Paradise Point, about eighty acres, then known as Hallock's Point, and still so named on sailors' charts because it had been in the Hallock family ever since a Hallock bought it from the Indians, was owned by my grandfather, Joseph Hallock. He also owned one-third of Little Hog Neck, now Nassau Point, besides his large farm at Hog Neck. He was one of the biggest landowners of his day. My grandfather sold forty acres of Paradise Point to Silas Horton for $1,000. Quite a contrast to what it is worth to-day. The property now belongs to Mr. Robert M. Searle.

Fortunately, my grandfather did not sell the remaining forty acres, to the south, with its one-third mile shore front, and we retain some of the original tract to-day, on which stand "The Bandbox" and Tom Currie-Bell's studio. The family sold, at what we then considered a good price, large shore-front plots, on which now stand the residences of Mr. Robert M. Searle, Mr. Chas. B. Byron, John S. Jenkins, Rev. Dr. Robert J. Kent and Mr. Robert Gilbert.

Our Present Home

In the year 1900 we decided that we could afford to build a home. With the advent of "Little Ann" our quarters over the *Traveler* office were rather

OUTSIDE THE "RED HOUSE"

Joseph and Ella Hallock's home on the corner of Main Road and Maple Lane was set back from the road, leaving plenty of space for gatherings on the front lawn. Here, Joseph, Ella (standing) and Ella's sister Grace are flanked by Ella and Cam Higgins.

cramped. I purchased a lot of Wm. Y. Fithian, corner of Main St. and Maple Lane, and Boss J. Edward Corey built my present residence. Many thought I was foolish to build so far back from the road, but I am very glad that I did. Then there were very few automobiles and not much traffic on the roads.

I remember that the first day we moved into our new home, Ann cried bitterly and "wanted to go home," but she soon became reconciled to her new surroundings after her mother had fed her with a banana, and I have never heard her express the wish to go back to the home where she was born. I had the house built for two families as my mother and sister Lucy lived with us until Lucy married Mr. Folk and they built their own home.

FOLK HOUSE, MAPLE LANE
Lucy married Albert A. Folk and built a house just down Maple Lane from where Joseph had built his home. The yellow brick house, named "Folkholm," had one of the loveliest gardens in Southold.

My Political Life and Views

Even before I became a voter, I was greatly interested in politics and made political speeches in the Garfield campaign when I was 19 years old. I have always been a strong Organization Republican, and it is very seldom that I have split my ticket. I served as a member of the Republican County Committee for eight years, was elected for three terms as Member of Assembly from the First Suffolk District and served for 25 years as Town Clerk of Southold Town. On my election to the Presidency of the Southold Savings Bank, I retired from active participation in politics.

I have always been ultra-conservative in my political views, as well as in other matters. I suppose many would say that I am "sot," and I guess they would not be far wrong in their diagnosis of my character. I suppose I inherited that tendency from my Puritan forbears. I have no sympathy with radical notions of any kind. Naturally, I have no use for the New Deal or its sponsors, whether they hold high or low positions. I am, like my hero Calvin Coolidge, strongly opposed to the Government interfering or being in business in competition with private capital. I admire and follow men of the type of Grover Cleveland, William McKinley, Charles Evan Hughes, Calvin Coolidge and Herbert Hoover. I consider Mr. Hoover to be the greatest man in this country. Grover Cleveland was a Democrat and I am a Republican, but I believe that Mr. Cleveland will go down in history as one of our greatest Presidents.

Theodore Roosevelt was Governor of New York when I served in the State Legislature, and I knew him well. I had little sympathy with his radical notions of reforming the Government when he became President, and when he broke with the Republican party, which had made him, and ran on the "Bull Moose" ticket in opposition to President Taft, thereby electing Woodrow Wilson, I was forever through with him.

—m—

President of
Southold Savings Bank

In 1900 I was elected a Trustee of the Southold Savings Bank, and served as a member of the Examining Committee, Second and First Vice President. In 1932, I was elected President of this well-known institution. This I consider the greatest honor that ever came to me. When I was a lad on my father's farm I had great respect for the Southold Savings Bank, its officers and trustees, especially the Treasurer, Henry Huntting. They say that fond parents think that some day their boy may be President of the United States.

I know that neither I nor my parents ever dreamed that I would some day fill the honorable position of President of the Southold Savings Bank.

Summing Up

There has been little continuity in these memoirs, and they have spun out much longer than I anticipated. I have endeavored to jot down such remembrances of long ago that I thought might be of interest to my daughter. It is with fond recollection that I recall the old days, full to the brim with hard work and yet spiced with lots of fun. Call them, if you will, "horse and buggy days," and who will say that those days did not make strong men and women, men and women of character and sturdy independence?

The young people then did not have a fraction of the pleasures of our present-day youth, and yet who will say that the boys and girls of yesterday did not have as much real fun in their simple lives? But we will have to admit that we older ones would not want to go back to the hardships and lack of conveniences of the former days. I guess we are getting soft. Then, instead of the electric light, we had the tallow-candle. Then, we went up-stairs to bed to our cold room instead of to the steam-heated room of today. Then, telephones, radios, automobiles, movies were unheard of, and a bath-room was a luxury only for the very rich. Instead of opening a tap for water, we would go and draw up "the old oaken bucket" from the well, filled to the brim with cold, sparking water. Instead of buying milk from the milkman, we would go out in the cold, frosty mornings and milk the cows. Instead of having sea-food brought to our doors, we would go down to the bays and creeks to dig, rake and fish for it. Instead of the short working hours of today, the morning sun would seldom find us in bed, and that same sun would be near its setting when we ceased the day's labors. No, we would not want to go back to the former days, much as we recall them with fond recollection.

Evening of Life

I am now seventy-six years old and in the "evening of life." I have witnessed many changes. The sad has been mixed with the gay. A sister, Georgianna; brother, Ben; father; mother; Mother Boldry and sister, Grace Boldry; and my dear wife Ella, with whom I lived in blessed fellowship for forty-five years, have passed on to the Better Land. My daughter Ann, son Tom Currie-Bell and sister Lucy are still with me to see to my comfort and happiness. With fond recollections of the dear departed ones, and with the love of those still with me, coupled with the esteem and respect of my fellow-men, God willing, I shall "carry on."

Our Family Life

Our family life was most pleasant and congenial. We were indeed a happy family. Seven children were born to my parents. My brother Clarence, sister Mary Jane and an infant daughter died at an early age before I was born.

My brother, Ben, some years older than me, attended Bridgehampton Academy and the Albany State Normal School. He taught school at Peekskill, N.Y., for one year, but not liking that profession, he entered the employ of C.B. Hewitt & Co., paper manufacturers and dealers of 48 Beekman St., N.Y. City, and remained a prized employee of that firm until his death at the age of 69 years. He had a very fine head for business. He married Miss Mary Denham of N.Y. City and raised a family of four children—George, Edna, Nellie and Ruth. For his second wife he married Miss Carrie Young of N.Y. City, who survives him.

The death of my sister Georgianna, at the age of 22 years, was a great blow to her family. She was a very bright, lovely girl and a fine musician. She inherited much of her father's mild and gentle disposition, as well as her mother's beautiful character. I well remember the good times we had together. She and my sister Lucy were greatly devoted to each other and were inseparable.

My father strained himself by some work on the farm when a young man and was never very strong, yet he was able to do much light work. As I have said before, he was one of Nature's Noblemen. He was of the old type. His word was as good as his bond. I never knew him to do a mean thing, and he could not, for that was entirely foreign to his nature. He was a true descendant of his Puritan ancestors, and yet with all their fine qualities of honesty and integrity, he was very mild and gracious. He died at the age of 73 years. I used to think he was a very old man, for he wore a full white beard, and yet at his death he was three years younger than I am now.

Like many another man, I owe a great debt to my mother. She, too, was of Puritan ancestry. Like her ancestors, she had very decided opinions of right and wrong. She was a very strong character and yet had one of the sweetest dispositions I ever knew. She was one of the grandest women who ever lived. She passed through lots of trouble, in that husband and five children were taken from her, and yet, through it all, she was always an optimist. She could always see the silver lining through the clouds. She had an unwavering faith in the goodness of God, and that sustained her through every trial. She died at the ripe old age of 95 years, with all her faculties unimpaired.

My sister Lucy, the youngest of the family, married Albert A. Folk, President of the Bank of Southold and Secretary of the Suffolk Co. Mutual Insurance Co., and they built a beautiful home on Maple Lane. There they, in company with my mother, passed a number of happy years until Mr. Folk passed on. Mr. Folk was a very able and conscientious business man, of Quaker descent. He was a great reader and especially well-informed, and had one of the finest private libraries in the County. My sister Lucy is now one of the prized members of our family and makes her home with us. The winter months we all spend in Florida, and Ann and Tom generally prolong their stay for six or seven months.

When the public library was started, with one accord the people said the position of librarian should be held by Lucy Hallock. She filled that position for a number of years until she was married, and she filled it extremely well. By extensive reading, tact, courtesy and a lovely disposition, she was well fitted for a librarian and was very popular with the patrons of the library. I will always hold in grateful remembrance the uniform kindness and thoughtful care Lucy had for our mother in her declining years. She was truly a wonderful daughter, and she is a deeply loved sister and aunt.

I well remember the advent of the coming of "Little Ann" to our rooms over the *Traveler* office. It was an anxious time, but it was soon turned to a most happy one. The skillful Dr. Hartranft and the capable nurse, Mrs. Anna Lehr, were in charge. To the fond parents' minds, the most lovely baby who ever lived grew up and prospered. The Hallock baby was greatly admired and loved as she was wheeled in her carriage through the village streets by her proud mother. It is a wonder that she was not spoiled, especially by her grandmother Hallock, for whom she could do no wrong.

When Ann was three years old she went with her father and mother to Albany, where I served three winters in the New York Legislature. The first winter we lived in Albany, and the following two winters we made our home with Ann's grandmother Boldry at Green Island—and to this grandmother, as was the case with the other, Ann was perfect. At Green Island Ann went to Kindergarten. When it came time to go to school, Ann's mother took her up to the Primary room. It was no use; Ann was so homesick that her mother gave it up as a bad job. The following year, despite protests on the part of Ann, her mother put her foot down and said Ann must go to school.

Very soon Miss Deale, who was a wonderful teacher, made Ann feel at home, and ever thereafter the young lady did not want to miss a day. She graduated as Salutatorian of her class at the Southold High School, under Prof. A.W. Symonds, entered and graduated at Vassar College and then took a post-graduate course in dramatics at Harvard College under the renowned Prof. Baker. She then took a course at the Leland Powers School of Oratory at Boston. On completing this course, she secured a very fine position as Dramatic Director of the Margaret Fuller Settlement House at Cambridge, Mass.[22]

At the end of eight years of very successful work there, she took a trip to Europe, traveling in England, Scotland, France, Belgium, Holland, Germany and Italy. On this trip she met the internationally known Scotch artist, Tom Currie-Bell. It was a case of love at first-sight. They carried on a steady correspondence, and, soon after Ann's return, Tom made a trip here at Christmas time so that the parents could see what manner of a man he was. He passed inspection all right, and Ella and I made only one condition to their marriage, and that was that as long as we lived they should make their home in this country. We felt that the great ocean was too wide a separation from our only child.

Ann and Tom were married the next June. Their married life has proved a most happy one. They spend about six months with me, and the other six they spend in the South, where Tom is very successful in his portrait-painting. While Tom is very noted as an artist, Ann inherits much of her mother's talent as a writer, and her compositions are greatly admired for the clarity of her style. She is truly a wonderful girl, both intellectually and in her wonderful personality. I have good reason to be proud of her and her talented husband. God bless them, and may they spend many happy and successful years together. As they may read these memories in later years, may they think of "Pop," who penned the lines with a loving hand.

Mother Boldry and sister Grace I shall always hold in loving remembrance. Mr. Boldry I never knew, as he died at an early age. He was a native of England, and was a veteran of our Civil War. I am told that he was a very patriotic American, an especially well-read man, and alive to all the topics of the day. Our family spent two winters with Mother Boldry and Grace while I was in the Legislature, at their pleasant home in Green Island on the Hudson River. Mother would make yearly visits to our home, and her stay with us was all too-short. She was a home-body, and while she dearly loved us, no place to her was like home.

Mother Boldry was an extremely alert, active and capable woman, despite her advancing years, and was mighty well informed on the affairs of the day. She loved flowers and took great pride in her garden. She had a beautiful personality and was most highly esteemed by all who knew her. Ann was named after her grandmother, Ann Boldry. Mrs. Boldry died at the age of 73 years, and sleeps beside her soldier-husband in the beautiful Troy Cemetery on the banks of the Hudson.

Grace, soon after her mother's death, came to Southold to make her home with us, and remained a prized member of our household until her death in June 1937, three days after her 78th birthday. She sleeps beside her sister in the Presbyterian Cemetery. Grace was one of the most active persons I ever knew. She seemed never to tire in good works. She was of great aid to Ella in her household duties, and carried on most successfully after her sister's death. She was greatly interested in the Sunshine Society,[23] and attended all its meetings. She was generous to a fault and extremely unselfish.

She loved the woods and water, and would spend weeks at a time at Ella's Bandbox at Paradise Point. It seemed a peculiarly happy and appropriate ending that the last afternoon she spent on earth was spent in the woods and by the bay she loved so well. As we sat in the woods by Tom's studio at the bay, she remarked to me how she loved to hear the waves lapping on the shore. In about an hour, just after we arrived home, she fell asleep and her spirit passed on to the Farther Shore.

GRACE BOLDRY

Grace Boldry, Ella Hallock's sister, came to live with the Hallocks on Maple Lane and became a valued family member. Here she stands by the garden gate in the early 1900s.

Families at Bay View (Hog Neck)

As Far Back as I Can Remember

The families at Bay View, commencing at the east end of the Main Road, all of them farmers, were:[24]

Mr. and Mrs. Gilbert Horton, Mr. and Mrs. Gilbert W. Horton and sons, Gilbert and Daniel. (Mr. Edwin H. Brown, present owner).

Mr. and Mrs. Ezra T. Beebe and sons, Daniel and Ezra, and daughters, Anna, Phoebe and Lizzie.

Mr. and Mrs. Albert Terry. (Wm. Akscin, present owner. This was the place where my grandfather, Joseph,[25] father, George, and myself were born. It was built by my great-grandfather Joseph. Mr. Terry soon sold the farm to a Mr. Burns and moved to Southold, next to the home of his son, Jonathan B. Terry.)

Mr. and Mrs. Luther Wells and sons, Edward and Frank (Trapp's place).

Mr. and Mrs. Alfred Wells and daughter, Ethie, who married Michael Fisher. (Former Edw. Mills place, now Arch Davis.)

Mr. and Mrs. Peter Gilbert Wells and sons, Daniel and Gilbert (house not there).

Mr. and Mrs. Benjamin Wells and daughter, Lydia (house not there).

Mr. and Mrs. Halsey Dickinson (my grandparents).

Mr. and Mrs. George Hallock and sons, Benjamin and Joseph (myself), and daughters, Georgianna and Lucy. (Howard Terry Estate. My uncle, J. Nelson Dickinson lived with us.)

Mr. and Mrs. S. Moses Terry and sons, Jesse, George Henry and Alvah, and daughter, Helen. (Jesse Terry Estate.)

Mr. and Mrs. Silas Horton and Mr. and Mrs. George W. Dayton, son Silas Austin and daughter, Mary Landon. (Mary Dayton, present owner.)

Mr. and Mrs. Austin Horton. (Mary Dayton, present owner. This is the second oldest house in Bay View and was built by a Horton, ancestor of Miss Dayton. Then came the old School House.)

Mr. and Mrs. William Wells (now Reydon).

Mr. and Mrs. Hiram Terry and son Gilbert. (This is now the Reydon Club House. It was originally the oldest house in Bay View and was built by my great-grandfather, Joseph Hallock.)[26]

Mrs. Esther Terry and Miss Jerusha Hallock, sisters. (Mr. Jones, present owner.)

Mr. and Mrs. David Horton and daughters, Addie, Mattie and Josephine. (Mrs. Addie Thorne, present owner).

Mr. and Mrs. Seth T. Wells and daughter, Stephania. (Mr. Harne, present owner. This farm was originally owned by my grandfather Joseph, and he called it "Hill Lot.")

Mr. and Mrs. Martin V.B. Gordon, son Arthur and daughter, Lillie. (Elsie Dickinson, present owner.)

Mr. and Mrs. Henry M. Beebe, son William and daughters, Alida, Emma, Ettie and Nancy.

In what we called "Woodpecker Neck" lived:

Mr. and Mrs. Richard Griswold, sons Henry, David and William, and daughters, Bessie, Cynthia and Mary. (Mrs. Griswold would come every Monday morning to do our washing and I would go after her and drive her home.)

Mr. and Mrs. Charles Davis and son, Augustus.

Miss Sarah Overton and Sam Robinson.

Mr. and Mrs. Oliver Overton.

And on the far west end lived "Long-Legged" Ezra Horton and his very short wife. He and Sam Robinson were great characters (This place was the last house in School Dist. No. 6—Bay View).

On Jacob's Lane lived:

Mr. and Mrs. Hector Horton.

Mr. and Mrs. Benjamin Horton, son Lawrence and daughters, Jamie, Aggie and Grace. (Mary Dayton, present owner of both of these.)

Mr. and Mrs. Charles E. Terry, son Charles Grant and daughter May. (Mr. Terry was a Veteran of the Civil War.)

On the North Side of the Neck lived:

Mr. and Mrs. Walter Hannabury, son Charles and daughters, Lelitia, Mary and Lizzie. (J.B. Coleman, present owner.)

Mr. and Mrs. Charles Rorke, sons, James, Charles, Cornelius and John, and daughters, Lettie and Anna.

Mr. and Mrs. Michael Young, sons, John and David, and daughters, Mary Louise, Clara, Carrie and Katie. (Mr. J. Shipulesk, present owner.)

Mr. and Mrs. Patrick Fogarty, son Martin and daughters, Nora and Julia.

Mr. and Mrs. Edward Fogarty and daughters, Annie and Sadie.

Mr. and Mrs. Augustus Dunkel and daughter, Mary. (Mrs. Edw. H. Brown, present owner.)

Mr. and Mrs. Grover Pease, son Preston and daughters, Sadie and Hattie (Goose Bay Estates).

All of these families except six, four Irish and two German, were of American stock, and for the far greater part, of Puritan ancestry. When I was a boy, I had never seen a native of Poland.

There have been great changes in the population of Bay View since I was a boy. The only old-time residents are Miss Mattie Wells and Miss Mary Landon Dayton. Now the homes are occupied by either city people or people of Polish descent.

Three-quarters of a century ago, there was not a single residence along Bay View's magnificent shore-front, on the North, East and West. Now, hundreds have their fine homes there. As a matter of fact, these homes are of recent origin. The large colonies of city people at Reydon Shores and Goose Bay Estates date back a very short time. The assessed valuation of Bay View has multiplied many times in recent years. Our fathers and grandfathers, in their wildest dreams, never pictured the Bay View of to-day. In those days Nature had been lavish in providing a beauty-spot, in coming years to be eagerly sought after by the city-dweller, but our forefathers did not realize it; neither did I. Their vision was bounded by their fertile farms. To my mind, there is no more beautiful spot on Earth than Bay View, with its bays, creeks and wooded roads, and its wonderful changing views across miles of rolling water.

Addenda: In speaking of old-time places in Bay View, I failed to mention a wind grist-mill that stood on a hill on the extreme North Side, overlooking Goose Creek and Southold Bay. This mill was purchased by a city party and moved to the South Side of Long Island.

Addenda

When I had finished writing the foregoing memoir, my daughter Ann said to me, "Pop, you want to keep right on writing. You will think of some more interesting incidents connected with your life." "No," I replied, "I guess I am through." She was right, for the following incidents have come to mind:

Our Vegetable Garden

Lying between our house and barn at Bay View was the vegetable garden. There we raised peas, string beans (Lima beans were unheard of), lettuce (not head), carrots, beets, radishes, a strawberry bed and, best and most profitable of all, an asparagus bed. I think we were the only ones in Bay View to have asparagus. For greens, we used to pick dock in the fields, and I never tasted any greens equal to it. We had hop vines, from which my mother made yeast. Our first green vegetables were from our garden. One would not have thought of buying them at the store; in fact, they were not there for sale.

In front of the garden, on the roadside, was a large mint bed. The children, on their way to and from school, would stop there and pick some. I can smell and taste that mint now. I thought it a great delicacy. The sweet-corn we raised in the farm lot, and when that was gone we used fodder-corn on the table, and that was not at all bad, though I suppose you would stick up your nose at it now. We raised plenty of pop-corn, and we would pop and eat it in the winter evenings. It was a pretty sight to see it pop in the corn-popper. We also would roast dried sweet-corn, with plenty of butter, in the spicler.[27]

Bread and Milk

We had plenty of milk, and a frequent dish was a bowl of home-made bread and milk, warm and fresh from the cow. I used to feast on it.

No Refrigerator

We had no ice-boxes or refrigerators then. The "ice-box" was down well. By a long rope we would lower, down well, in pails, milk and butter and other things we wanted to keep cool. Occasionally, in drawing up a pail of water, I would upset the pail of milk, and then the water would have a milky appearance.

Southold Business Men

In the following list, names in parentheses show the present occupants: Frank Wells of Bay View, who picked up eggs, had a room in his house in which he kept a few simple groceries which he would barter for eggs. But for the most part we did our trading at Southold when we went to the Post Office (across from Soldiers' Monument) kept by "Johnny" Huntting. The meat markets were kept by Hezekiah Jennings (building now stands in rear of Mrs. Annie Jennings' lot) and Frank Landon (Henry L. Jewell). The grocery stores were kept by Charles S. Tillinghast (Mrs. Charlotte Overton), Sherburne A. Beckwith (Miss Willa Hagerman and Arthur Gagen) and F.L. Judd. Wm. C. Albertson was manager & later bought the business. Chas. Merrill was the first owner (Albert W. Albertson).

The general store, dry goods and groceries, was kept by William Wells and his son, J. Albert Wells (Southold Savings Bank). They also kept the only Hotel in the same building, later kept by F.L. Judd, later by Isaac Billard, later by Charles Hannabury, later by Kent and John Steffens, Theo. Hoinkis. It was sold to Southold Savings Bank and torn down. Richard Carpenter, the tailor, had his shop there. J. Albert Wells later sold his store business to Prince Bros., Henry W. and Orrin A., Henry and G. Frank Hommel later built the Brick Store,[28] now housing the post office and Roper's Restaurant. Mr. Prince had his general store in the east side and Mr. Hommel his shoe store in the west side. The Odd Fellows for many years had their lodge room in the upper story over Mr. Hommel's, and the Grange met in the room over Mr. Prince's.

J.B. Terry carried on a general produce business and had a store at Southold Wharf (Town Harbor Park). The blacksmiths were Henry C. Cleveland, later Cleveland and Glover (Frank Gagen, who has the original shop) and Daniel Terry (rear of C.F. Kramer lot). The cobblers were Godfrey Hahn (Joost Building) and G. Frank Hommel (Post Office). Jerry Singley (Mullen's Garage) and Samuel Eldredge (Petty's blacksmith shop) were the wheelwrights. Charles Barth (The Weckesser store) sold beer.

Just before I was born, there was an iron foundry, corner of Railroad Ave. at Traveler St. (Koke Bros.). I can remember when Henry G. Howell built his drug store (David Rothman). Albertson Case had his law office in one rear room, and the Southold Lyceum Association had its library in

THE BRICK STORE, MAIN ROAD
When first built in 1874, the building had Henry W. Prince's Store on the right and G. Frank Hommel's shoe store on the left. Upstairs was the Odd Fellows Hall and later the Southold Grange.

the other rear room. The Sons and Daughters of Temperance, and later Banner Lodge IOGT[29] had their lodge room up-stairs. I was at one time a member of Banner Lodge, and after Lodge the boys would go across the street to the ice-cream saloon in the basement of the Brick Store and have a dish of ice cream before our walk home. The first proprietor of the ice-cream saloon was Philip Cantermen, followed by Capt. Bill Maynard and H.G. Booth.

The *Long Island Traveler* was first published at Cutchogue in 1871 by Rev. Nathan Hubbell and L.F. Terry. Mr. Terry moved the office to Southold, where the drug store is now. M.B. Van Dusen purchased the paper and moved the building to where it now stands. The east part of the building is the original office.

My Religious Belief

True to the teachings of my mother, when I was a young man I joined the Methodist Church, which I have always faithfully attended and am still a member. I may not be a Liberal in my political views, but I am decidedly so in matters of religion. I believe there is great good in every sect, in every religion. If a man is living a clean life, doing the best he knows how and with love and charity for his neighbor, I care not whether he be Protestant, Catholic, Jew, Mormon, Mohamedan, Buddist, a follower of Zoaraster, an Indian worshipping the Great Spirit, or the native in Darkest Africa with his strange gods. All, to my mind, are groping after God, the Great Master of the Universe. I suppose that is the reason why I cannot get up much enthusiasm for Foreign Missions. I do not wish you to imply that I do not fully believe in Jesus Christ and in his Divinity. I do most implicitly, and am certain that he is the Greatest Teacher who ever lived. To my mind, there is no one on the same plane. He towers above all others. He is perfection. He is Divine. "The Blessed's" of the Beatitudes, as expounded in the Sermon on the Mount, are the very highest type of religion. Theological creeds matter little to me. But—it is not for me to say that sincere followers of other religions have not as good a right to their opinions as have I. I do not consider it my province to endeavor to mould others' opinions.

If this be heresy, then I am a heretic. At least I am true to myself. Do you know, on the whole, I do not consider myself unorthodox on the essential verities of religion. I simply have respect for the other fellow's viewpoint, for his belief, for his religion.

—m—

The First Automobile

The first automobile in town was driven by John Howell. John was ever a daring soul, and he seemed to be willing to take his life in his hands as he sped along our village streets at the reckless speed of ten miles an hour. Dr. J.H. Marshall, who had a summer home at the Sound, had a large red car, and he and his three young daughters, May, Georgia and Phoebe, could often be seen in the village in their car. Our townspeople would line the streets in open-eyed wonder at these strange vehicles and their reckless drivers.

But their wonder was as nothing compared to the fright of the horses. The mildest-tempered horse, which had never been known to shy at anything, would try to climb a tree to get out of the way of John's and Doctor's devil-wagons, as they chugged along with the noise of a brass band and spouting steam and fire. Many cusses were hurled by the drivers at our two friends. If the frantic team could be held in the road, the driver gave the auto little leeway and fervently hoped he could crowd it into the ditch.

Soon Fords became fashionable, and it was no uncommon sight to see many cars alongside the road for repairs. I wonder if John still has that car. I know it outlasted many of modern make. He should keep it as a relic of past generations.

Rev. Wm. H. Lloyd, of blessed memory, who came to Southold to fill the pulpit of the Presbyterian church the month and year that Ann was born, had a white, three-seated automobile of ancient vintage. I think nearly every boy in town learned to drive in this car. The car remained one of the landmarks of the village for many years.

Fellow-Scholars at Bay View

My fellow-scholars at Bay View were:

Gilbert Horton
Daniel and Phoebe Beebe
Rowland, Ezra and Lizzie Beebe
George H., Edward, Frank and Gilbert Wells
George Fanth [Ford] (father of Senator Ford)
my brother Ben and sister Georgianna
Alvah Terry
Gilbert Terry
Howard, Daniel and Minnie Hallock
Josephine and Mattie Horton
Stephania Wells
Arthur and Lillie Gordon
William Beebe
Alida Beebe Clark
Emma Beebe Young
Ettie Beebe Tuthill
Nancy Beebe Boisseau
David, William, Cynthia and Mary Griswold
Lawrence and Aggie Horton Van Nort
Charles Hannabury
Letitia and Mary Hannabury Mahoney
John and David Young
Mary Louise Young Dickinson
Clara Young Hahn
Carrie Young Hallock
Annie Rorke

Fellow-Students at Southold Academy

My fellow-students at Southold Academy, under Prof. James R. Robinson, were:

Minnie Terry Smith
Hattie Terry
Nellie Huntting Bly
Tillie Edwards
Jessie Boisseau Wells
Annie Howell Terry
Carrie Judd
Ella Foster
Annie Fithian Jackson
Kittie Williams Case
Lucy Goldsmith Brown
Annie Tuthill Phillips
Egenia Hallock
Mary Richmond Fitz
Flora Overton Appleby
Nellie Thomas Fordham
Frank J. Wells

Jos. C. Case
J. Alvin Squires
George W. Fitz
George R. Jennings
Alvah Terry
Gilbert Horton
Howard Hallock
John A. Wilbur
Frank N. Tillinghast
Charles L. Young
Charles Richmond
William Booth
Jay Robinson
Edward Maxwell
William Conway
Clarence Wilcox

My Bay View Scholars

The year I taught school at Bay View my scholars were:

Daniel H. Horton
Neevie and Jesse Wells
Minnie Wells Maier
Eda Wells Kramer
Cephar Jefferson
Nathaniel Beebe
Augustus Davis
Charles Grant Terry
May Terry Newbold
Charles, Cornelius, John, Lettie and Anna Rorke
James and Neil Rorke
Martin, Nora, Julia and Sadie Fogarty
Sadie and Hattie Pease

and an Overton boy, whom I taught his ABC's in the old-fashioned way.

Daniel Horton was my most advanced scholar. I remember how I taught him book-keeping, in which he took a great interest. Notwithstanding his brightness, I will venture to say that neither of us dreamed then that some day the teacher would be President and the pupil Vice President and Member of the Finance Committee of "Henry Huntting's Savings Bank." His father and my father were great friends. They were both gentlemen of the old school. I can pay them no higher compliment. Would there were more men of the same type!

Our Pets

Our first pet—or I would be more correct in saying Ella's first pet, and that is true of the pets that followed—was a large stray cat that Ella fed, and it lost no time in adopting her. That cat would follow Ella like a dog, and when she called on neighbors, would wait until its mistress had finished her call and then would follow her back home.

Then came Gypie, a small bull-dog, that belonged to Michael Stelzer, a neighbor across the street. It came to the door and seemed hungry, and Ella, out of the goodness of her heart, fed it—not on dog-biscuit, but most bountifully. That dog lost no time in coming here daily for its meals, and very soon it decided to make its permanent headquarters at our hospitable home. Mr. Stelzer became disgusted with the attitude of Gypie, said it would not stay home, and if we wanted the dog enough to pay the license—for he would not—we could have it. Ella, with thankful heart, accepted the gift, and I promptly paid the $2.25 license fee. That faithful little dog slept in the best-cushioned chair in the house and never went hungry. While it liked us all, it worshipped Ella, and would follow her wherever she went. When it became so old and feeble that we had to send for Dr. Case to come and chloroform it, Ella cried like a baby—and there were also tears in Ann's and my eyes, for we all loved it.

I had a flock of hens, and Ella soon adopted them as her own and would always want to let them out of the pen so they could run around and pick grass. She dearly loved eggs, and she also loved the producers of those eggs. I would never kill a hen. I had hens in my flock that were at least ten years old and had long outlived their usefulness as egg-producers. All my hens died a natural death, old age being the cause.

One night, during the stay of Ann and Tom at Southampton, where Tom was painting portraits, they went to Hampton Bays to a church raffle. There they were lucky enough to draw a young white duck. Tom said it would be a great joke on "Pop" to give him that duck, so a few days after, when they came home, they brought the duck and put it in the hen-roost with the hens. They told me they heard a noise in the hen-roost and I had better take the lantern and go out and investigate. This I did, and I was some surprised to see that duck making itself at home with the hens. Thereafter it would always go around with the hens, though it seemed to have one or two special favorites.

GYPIE

Gypie, "a small bull-dog," had belonged to a neighbor but adopted the Hallocks as his family. Here he poses with Ann and her Aunt Lucy.

Ella would feed and water that duck, and have a large pan filled with water for its bath. No matter how busy she was reading or writing, she would stop to see that duck perform and waddle across the lawn. When Ella went out doors, the duck was sure to follow her. When the duck began to lay eggs, and it proved a prolific layer, Ella was both proud and happy, and she feasted on ducks' eggs. It was some time before it laid, and we supposed it was a drake. Imagine my surprise when I found a duck's egg in the hen's nest. That duck, like the hens, died of old age, to the sorrow of us all. We never had another, for we knew no duck could take its place in our affections.

When I was a small boy, I had a pet lamb that I was very fond of.

Methodist Church Steeple

During the heaviest storm that ever visited Southold (the Great Blizzard), the Methodist Church steeple blew down. Rather than make the necessary repairs, the Methodists decided to build the present, handsome church-edifice. The old church was moved back and turned part way around, and is now the present Sunday School room.

Under the old church was a high basement, and that was the Sunday School room then. In order to enter the church you had to ascend about ten steps. All during my boyhood and young manhood days I attended this old church. Among the leading members were:

Mr. and Mrs. Hezekiah Jennings
Mr. and Mrs. Sherburne A. Beckwith
Mr. and Mrs. S. Bailey Corey
Mr. and Mrs. Eli W. Howell
Mr. and Mrs. Lewis H. Tuthill
Mr. and Mrs. Franklin N. Terry
Mr. and Mrs. Wm. C. Albertson
Mrs. Frederick Terry
Mrs. George Hallock
Mrs. Henry M. Beebe
Mr. and Mrs. E. Lucky Boisseau
Ezra Boisseau
Capt. Watts Overton
Samuel Weeks
Mr. and Mrs. Baldwin J. Payne
Capt. Orrin Prince
Henry W. Prince
Mr. Augustus Terry
Mrs. Jane Skidmore
Mr. and Mrs. John Koin

E. Lucky Boisseau was the leader of the choir. The first pastor I remember was Rev. Mr. Lyons. Other early pastors, in my day, were William H. Russell, John Simpson, Edwin Warriner, Theodore C. Beach (the greatest pulpit orator in the history of the church), John Pilkington, George Taylor, A.S. Graves and Ephraim Watt.

J. EDWARD COREY

J. Edward Corey stands in the doorway of his shop, circa 1887. "Boss" Corey built the Hallock home on Maple Lane, now owned by the Southold Historical Society.

Boss J.E. Corey was the builder of the new church and Frank Poltinger was the painter. It was a great day when the church was dedicated. Bishop John F. Hurst, the greatest scholar in Methodism, was the preacher. Rev. Dr. Whitaker offered the prayer. Rev. Henry E. Hiler was pastor of the church.

The Methodists held their first meetings in private houses, mostly at a Mrs. Peters' on Youngs Ave. Occasionally a circuit preacher, who covered most of Long Island, would be present and expound the Gospel of Free Will. But for the most part, class-leaders would be in charge of the meetings. The first Methodist Church stood on the corner of Main St. and Boisseau Ave. For 150 years and more, the Presbyterian Church, founded in 1640, had been the only Church in Southold or on Long Island, outside of Brooklyn and Jamaica, where were Dutch Reformed Churches. The Catholics and Universalists did not have churches here until many years after the Methodists.

Legislative Work

I enjoyed very much the three winters I spent in Albany as a member of the New York State Assembly. Three terms were all they would give a member then, no matter how good he was. I think I did fairly good work for my constituents. I introduced and had passed a bill making an appropriation for the building of the east cement sea-wall at Orient, so as to protect the road from encroachment by LI Sound. I tell folks that is my monument. I was also instrumental in securing an appropriation for the benefit of the farmer. At every session, bills were introduced inimical to the net fishermen of my district. I was successful in defeating every such bill, and thus won the gratitude of my fishermen friends.

At the request of the Audubon Society, I introduced and had passed a bill for the protection of sea-gulls. There had been no restriction to the killing of these beautiful birds, and they had been killed by the million for the milliner trade. When the bill was passed, I went to Governor Theodore Roosevelt and asked him to sign it so it would become a law. "Sign it," he said, "of course I'll sign it as soon as it reaches me. That's a bully good bill," and he gave me a resounding whack on my shoulders.

They say there is lots of corruption in politics, but during all my stay in Albany I was never approached by a lobbyist. Once a fellow-member told me if I would go see a certain party I could get $2,000 if I would agree to vote against a certain very meritorious bill. I told him my vote was not for sale, and when the bill came up for passage I promptly voted for it.

When a closed roll-call is made on some important bill, the Assembly doors are closed and guarded, and no member can either leave or get in. The Sergeant-at-Arms is directed to round up all absent members and bring them before the bar of the house. An absent member is liable to a fine of $25. One day, not knowing that a closed roll-call was to be made, I was showing Mr. Harry Lee of Riverhead the sights of the capitol building. I spied the Sergeant-at-Arms making a bee line for me, and he said I was under arrest and must come with him before the bar of the house, that a closed roll-call was on. On my being brought before the bar, the Republican leader moved that I be excused. The Speaker put the question, and not a member voted to excuse me. When the "No's" were called for, a thunderous "No," that shook the rafters, went up. The Speaker, without turning a hair, declared that the motion to excuse me had been carried, and I was saved from turning over $25 of my hard earned salary to the State Treasury.

Flock of Hens

Like every other farmer, my father had a large flock of hens. They had a nice, comfortable hen-roost, but their pen was all out-doors, and they wandered at will.

We did not go in then for a particular strain, as they do now. Those fowl were certainly a mixed or mongrel breed, and every color of the rainbow. Every known fowl, from the large brahma to the small bantam, was represented. If we wanted to mix them up still more, we would trade a couple of our roosters for a neighbor's male birds. Our roosters did not take kindly to the visitors' coming on their domain, and there would ensue a cock-fight that beat anything I saw in Havana.

Our hens could not boast of a pedigree a mile long, but they were strong and healthy and were good layers. The egg-money purchased all the groceries, we had plenty of eggs to eat with ham and sausage, and there was still money left. The roosters found their way to the oven. Incubators and brooders were unheard of then. The mother-hen raised the chickens in the good old-fashioned way.

Barefoot Boy

"Barefoot boy, with cheeks of tan" was a fit description of myself. All of the boys and some of the men went barefoot in summer. The soles of my feet were like leather. In my day, girls did not go without shoes and stockings. Aunt Esther Terry used to tell me how she would walk barefoot to church to save her shoes, taking her shoes and stockings with her, and just before she arrived at church she would sit down by the roadside and put them on. In my boyhood it would have been considered indecent for a girl to show either bare or stockinged legs, as they do to-day.

And the dresses either trailed in the dust or were not higher than the shoe-tops. The coming of short dresses I consider one of the most sensible innovations of fashion, even if it does show a nice leg, and that is nothing to be ashamed of. But in the old days the people would have been shocked at the display. I well remember the great furor when the "Black Crook" was shown on the New York stage. To-day those costumes would be considered the height of modesty.

Peddlers

One of the exciting events of farmer days was the occasional visit of a peddler. The first peddler I remember was a Mr. Dee. He carried on foot, attached to a strap over his back, two tin boxes. These were filled with a few dress goods, pins, needles, scissors, knives, forks, spoons, thread, jewelry and some trinkets. He would often stay at our house for meals, and sometimes over-night. My mother would always trade out the price of his meal, 25 cents for a meal and 50 cents for lodging and breakfast. Another foot-peddler, with similar goods, was a Mr. Salter. Still another was a Mr. Sargent, who carried jewelry exclusively. I still have a big silver watch that my father bought me.

John Korn came around in his wagon, filled with dry goods, and my mother always made some simple purchase. Henry Ford came around with his wagon, filled with tinware of all kinds. My mother would save for months rags, old worn-out clothing and paper, and these she would trade for a dipper, pail or pan. With the advance of civilization, the traveling peddler has become a thing of the past, and a picturesque figure is no more seen trudging our streets.

Speaking of John Korn, who was one of the last of our peddlers, reminds me of the day he called at our home over the *Traveler* office, when Ann was a little baby. In coming in with dress goods to show Ella, he left the door open, and Ann, unseen by us, creeped on her hands and knees to the head of the stairs and rolled down the entire length. Fortunately she was not hurt, but was a little scared at this new experience. Not so with her fond parents. They were scared out of a year's growth. Mr. Korn wanted to complete his sale, but Ella would have no more to do with him. She gave all her attention to "Little Ann," and she was soon all right, none the worse for her tumble. They say that drunken men and babies are seldom hurt by a fall, as they do not try to save themselves.

Mills

There used to be a wind-mill, for the grinding of flour and feed, at Mill Hill,[30] where Mr. D.V. Barnes' residence is now. Rene Villifreu, a Frenchman, was the miller. I can remember when this mill was burned down. There was also a wind-mill on the north side of Bay View, overlooking Goose Creek. In the early days there was another wind-mill at Town Harbor. There was a water-mill at Mill Creek, the miller being Edward H. Terry, who later moved to Patchogue and was succeeded by David J. Conklin and a Mr. Buckley.

I remember taking grists to the mills at Mill Hill and Mill Creek, and later to the Inlet Mill at Peconic, Gilbert Terry being the miller. James Allen built a large mill at Greenport, and I occasionally took grists there. The flour made in those old mills was not as white and refined as now, but the loaves of home-made bread, baked by my mother, were mighty tasty, and I could get away with many thick slices, either spread with home-made butter, molasses or molasses sugar.

Afterword

The Joseph N. and Ella Boldry Hallock house on Maple Lane and the Main Road was built in 1900–01. Builder: J. Edward Corey. Architect: John R. Higgins, cousin of Mrs. Hallock, and assisted by C.P. Tuthill. They moved over with their one child, Ann, and Joseph N.'s mother, Maria Jane Dickinson Hallock (Mrs. George Hallock, wife [widow] of George Hallock of Bay View or Hog Neck) and Joseph N.'s sister, Lucy (later, Lucy Hallock Folk, wife of Albert A. Folk).

This house became known as the Hallock home in Southold Village at the beginning of the twentieth century. Ann Hallock Currie-Bell inherited this house on her father's decease, October 1, 1942.

Ann Hallock Currie-Bell (daughter)

Picking Pears
Joseph Hallock was an enthusiastic gardener. Here, at seventy-eight, he is not too old to stand on top of the garage in order to harvest his pears.

Notes

1. The house still exists on the north side of Main Bayview Road, just east of Midland Parkway.
2. The two houses on this property also still stand, in front of the North Fork Sign Co. at 11185 Main Bayview.
3. The Bay View schoolhouse, built circa 1822, was a stone's throw from Hallock's home, across the road and just east of the Jacob's Lane triangle. It is now part of the Southold Historical Society complex on the Main Road.
4. Southold Academy, on the east side of Horton's Lane, operated from 1867 to 1907. It is now Academy Printing.
5. Daylight Savings.
6. Also spelled "Hashamomuck," it is a swampy area on the Southold-Greenport border. The very first area settlers lived here, harvesting pine trees for turpentine.
7. He calls it this because Mr. Huntting was the bank's treasurer for so many years. It was even originally housed in his own home.
8. Brushes' Hill was located near the holdings of the Corey Family on Hog Neck.
9. "The Bandbox" came into existence later, built as a retreat by Joseph and his wife Ella. It was moved to Paradise Point Road and still stands.
10. The wharf was demolished in 1954. Only the concrete wall near the shore remains.
11. The Oaklawn Estate, sixty acres in total, was bounded by Main Road, Wells and Oaklawn Avenues and Jockey Creek. The racetrack was down by the creek, as its name indicates.
12. The two Whitakers mentioned here were father and son. Dr. Epher Whitaker (1820–1916) was the longtime minister of the Presbyterian

Church and wrote a history of Southold. His son, William Force Whitaker (1853–1916), whose preaching career was in New Jersey, also died in 1916, just months before his father (who, ailing, never knew of the death of his son).

13. These good friends lived in Peconic, where Frank was a well-known milliner. Minnie wrote poetry and an occasional article for the *Traveler*.

14. M.B. Van Dusen was the second owner of the paper (first published in Cutchogue in 1871). He moved it to its current Traveler Street location in Southold in 1882.

15. The lowest-ranking apprentice at a printing establishment, the printer's devil got his name from the nature of his work. Mixing tubs of ink and fetching type inevitably stained him black with printing ink.

16. Due north of the town of Montauk, and an extension of Block Island Sound.

17. Free and Accepted Masons.

18. "The Run." The Run is where Jockey Creek went under Route 25 (Main Road) near Ackerly Pond Road, where Southold Marina is today.

19. This was a difficult word to translate from the original text. The name "Yaphet" refers to the Biblical story of Noah. Yaphet was one of Noah's three sons and founder of one of the three great races of the world.

20. Belmont Hall was also demolished in 1954. It stood on the south side of Main Road diagonally opposite Southold Library, where a parking lot is now.

21. In East Cutchogue, it separates Richmond Creek and Hog Neck Bay.

22. Margaret Fuller (1810–1850) was an American journalist, transcendentalist and women's rights advocate. The Margaret Fuller Settlement House, founded in 1902 and housed in her birthplace, still operates, providing family services to immigrants.

23. The Sunshine Society, still in existence today, seeks contributions of walkers, wheelchairs and other equipment for the ill and infirm, and then loans them out.

24. In parentheses, Joseph Hallock adds: "In this list I have named the children, but many of them, including my sisters, Georgianna and Lucy, were not born when I first remember the parents and the homes in which they lived."

25. A note by daughter Ann Currie-Bell reads: "This Joseph 2nd was born 1780 (see Hallock Genealogy). Therefore the house must have been built previous to that by his father, Joseph 1st, who apparently had moved down from the 1st Hallock House to live by that time (the 1st Hallock House being Reydon Club House with the smaller house [Aunt Esther & Aunt Jerusha])."

26. In another note, Ann makes the point that Joseph Hallock I was the first Hallock to live in Bay View, but not the first to own land there. His father, Zerrubabel, had willed the property to him.
27. This item has not been identified.
28. Built in 1874, it is now known as the Prince Building and houses the offices and archives of the Southold Historical Society.
29. International Order of Good Templars.
30. Mill Hill was the D.V. Barnes residence in 1937.

Index